The Grandeur of God

The Grandeur of God

A Theological and Devotional Study
of the Divine Attributes

C. Samuel Storms

Foreword by S. Lewis Johnson

BAKER BOOK HOUSE
Grand Rapids, Michigan 49506

ISBN: 0-8010-8254-4

Library of Congress
Catalog Card Number: 84-73200

Scripture quotations are taken from the *Holy Bible: New International Version*, © 1978 by the New York International Bible Society, used by permission of Zondervan Bible Publishers.

Printed in the United States of America

To three men who shaped my life . . .

Russell McKnight, whose loving patience and faithful teaching of God's Word first opened my eyes to the sovereignty of divine grace.

S. Lewis Johnson, whose theological excellence and friendship provided both godly example and personal encouragement.

And, especially, **Charles Storms,** my father (now with the Lord), whose life and love taught me what a genuine knowledge of God really is.

Contents

Foreword, S. Lewis Johnson, Jr.   9

Preface   13

1 The Christian's Proper Boast: *The Knowledge of God*   17

2 God Is What He Has! Or Is He? *Essence and Attribute*   33

3 One + One + One = One? *Trinitarianism*   47

4 His Eye Is on the Sparrow: *Omniscience*   61

5 Here, There, and Everywhere: *Omnipresence*   85

6 God and Round Triangles: *Omnipotence*   97

7 Great Is Thy Faithfulness: *Immutability*   107

8 How Sweet the Sound: *Grace*   117

9 John 3:16—Just What *Does* It Mean? *Love*   129

   Conclusion: *Rejoice in This Perfect Beauty!*   149

   Appendix A: *The Development of Trinitarianism in the Early Church*   153

   Appendix B: *The Sovereignty of God and Process Theism*   173

Foreword

Modern evangelicalism, with its current fads and theological fancies, apparently finds all it needs in "possibility thinking" and "prosperity theology." We are told we can manage all our problems. "If it's going to be, it's up to me" is the slogan of our Me Generation.

The fatal weakness of all this trivialization of biblical theology is its neglect of the fundamental truth that the ultimate solution to our needs and problems lies in God and His Word. As one of God's ancient men, Hosea, the Prophet of Unconditional Love, put it, "From Me is thy fruit found" (cf. 14:8). That's just this man-of-God's way of saying that the problems and puzzles of life find their solution in right thoughts about God and in a consequent commitment to Him as He has revealed Himself in His Word.

I know that it is common to use the word *theology* to denote irrelevance because—if it can be made to stick— then all of our fads, fancies, and self-promoting propaganda can go unchallenged and, indeed, unexamined. Better men and minds, however, will not sell their birthright for this mess of pottage.

Benjamin Breckinridge Warfield, one of the greatest of the Christian thinkers of the twentieth century, said it so pithily and well, "What, after all, is peculiar to Christianity is not the religious sentiment and its working, but its message of salvation—in a word, its doctrine. To be indifferent to doctrine is thus but another way of saying we are indifferent to Christianity ("The Right of Systematic Theology," *Selected Shorter Writings*, ed. by John E. Meeter [Nutley: Presbyterian and Reformed Publishing Company, 1973] II pp. 226-27).

That brings me to this book of good doctrine, of which these comments form a Foreword. The author, Samuel Storms, one of our promising young men in evangelicalism, is a former student of mine, now a colleague in the work of the ministry, and a long-time friend. During thirty-five years of teaching in theological seminaries, I have had a number of excellent students, and they have contributed much to me, but C. S. Storms has been one of the very best, and I have learned significantly from him.

As a Christian servant, he has not only been a dedicated, dependable, and fruitful servant of our Lord, but also extremely effective in the communication of God's truth, a marriage of gift and talent not often seen.

As a Christian scholar, he is blessed with a fine, logical and perceptive mind, devoid of the obfuscations of many of us. On surpassingly transcendent themes he writes with clarity and simplicity. I predict a bright future for him in whatever course of ministry God may lead him.

His book should have a warm response from thinking evangelicals. It is about God and theology and is both relevant and vital. The reader may not agree with all of Storms's points, but will acknowledge that they are cogently argued, and with spiritual warmth.

The author does not apologize for writing yet another book about God, contending that He is, in the author's word, "inexhaustible." He is right, and I wish for this work a good reading by the Christian public. God will still be just as inexhaustible after the finishing of it, for He is the infinite God. But if we read it, we will all understand in a fresh and clearer way why He is inexhaustible.

Henry Nelson Wieman is said to have described the difference between a philosopher and a theologian in this way: "A philosopher is like a dietician, and a theologian is like a good cook." Well, although I am not taken with Wieman's distinction, I know that the contents of this theologian's book make for good food. And while our giddy age may in its shallow and fanatically perverse way yield to the *odium theologicum*, like a child to castor oil, *The Grandeur of God* will prove to be healing medicine for the many who read and ponder its message.

S. Lewis Johnson, Jr.

Professor of Biblical and Systematic Theology
Trinity Evangelical Divinity School
Deerfield, Illinois

Minister
Believers Chapel
Dallas, Texas

Preface

This is a book about God. That might sound pretty dull to some. After all, what could possibly compare with the excitement generated by reading the latest attempt to identify the Antichrist or being told (and shown!) why one's sex life is not what it should be? I do not mean to be flippant, but the doctrine of God, sad to say, is simply not in fashion today. He (or "She" or "It"—if the National Council of Churches gets its way!) seems to have lost His relevance. People are more concerned with learning how to accept themselves, how to defeat depression, how to cope with their children, and "how to" just about anything else that strikes their fancy. I must confess right now that this is not a "how to" book. It is a "who" and "what" book. My purpose is singular and simple: *Who* is God and *what* is He like? If that does not interest you, then you should not waste your time reading further. On the other hand, if you sincerely believe that loving God is more important than loving yourself, and that the solutions to life's many crises are to be found in God-centered, not human-focused, thinking, read on. . . .

However, before you proceed to the first chapter, one more preliminary comment is in order. A lot of people in the last 1,900 years have written about God: His existence, attributes, and saving acts. Each author wrote in the belief that his or her contribution filled a gap in the literature currently available. Many of these books are still in print today. The first volume I read which was devoted exclusively to the nature of God was A. W. Pink's *The Attributes of God*. An excellent, though brief study, it whetted my appetite for more. And *more* is what I got: 802 pages of microscopic print by Stephen Charnock! This book, *The Existence and Attributes of God*, was written in the seventeenth century. It is massive, meticulous, and (to be perfectly honest) a bit too much for the average Christian to read from cover to cover. Not as long but more technical is Herman Bavinck's *The Doctrine of God*, a goldmine of theological, philosophical, and biblical data on the Deity. It was, however, J. I. Packer's *Knowing God*, published in 1973, which influenced and informed my understanding of God more than anything else I have previously read. Over the past several years I have recommended Packer's book not only to aspiring students of theology but also to those whose daily burdens could best be eased by adopting a decidedly theocentric perspective on life. This is but to say that *Knowing God* is eminently practical precisely because it is eminently theological.

Why, then, it may be asked, have I chosen to write yet another book on the doctrine of God? The reason is simple: *God is inexhaustible.* He is the one subject on which the last word will never be said! Notwithstanding this consideration, I have made a studied effort not to duplicate what Packer and others have written. For example, I purposely refrain from discussing the jealousy and wrath of God because in my opinion Packer's treatment is entirely adequate. Again, that is not to say that the final word has been uttered, only that *I* cannot think of anything more or better to say concerning those two divine attributes. On the other hand, I have devoted considerable attention to aspects of the doctrine of God not directly addressed by Packer (e.g., the relation between God's essence and attributes, triunity, omniscience, omnipotence, omnipresence, and certain problems relating to immutability). Even in areas of overlap I have focused on other truths relating to the attribute in question (as with the grace and love of God, the sovereignty and distinguishing nature of which receive special emphasis).

My prayer, then, is that this brief exploration into the most blessed of all subjects will prove useful and edifying to the believing community and, above all, glorifying to Him whom to know is life eternal.

I would like to take this opportunity to mention several people who have contributed, directly or indirectly, to this book.

First, I want to express my gratitude to the Elders of Believers Chapel, Dallas, Texas, for their support and encouragement. Their willingness to grant me the freedom and time to pursue this study will forever be appreciated.

Second, the members of my class, "the Doctrine of God," in the Believers Bible Institute are worthy of special notice. Their careful scrutiny of the manuscript and critical comments proved invaluable in the preparation of the final draft.

Finally, no words can adequately describe the debt I owe to Ann, my wife, whose patience and encouragement during the writing of this book bordered on the divine!

The Christian's Proper Boast

The Knowledge of God

I t is a tragic commentary on the condition of evangelicalism today that the author of a book on the excellencies of God should feel compelled to offer a justification for writing it. In fact, it strikes me as so incredibly tragic that I have decided to resist the compulsion and assume (I hope not mistakenly) that there are enough Christian people who believe that God is worth knowing to warrant my effort.

The Only Thing Worth Knowing

Of course, no thinking Christian would dare say that God is not worth knowing, for as Jeremiah has so pointedly informed us, He is, comparatively speaking, the *only* thing worth knowing: "This is what the LORD says: 'Let not the wise man boast of his wisdom or the strong man boast of his strength or the rich man boast of his riches, but let him who boasts boast about this: that he understands and knows me, that I am the LORD, who exercises kindness, justice and righteousness on earth, for in these I delight,' declares the LORD" (Jer. 9: 23–24). In similar fashion, Jesus himself declared: "Now this is eternal life: that they may know you, the only true God, and Jesus Christ, whom you have sent" (John 17:3).[1]

Notwithstanding this unmistakable theocentric focus in Holy Scripture, "contemporary man," observes Carl Henry, "seems to have lost God's address. But that is not all. He is unsure how to pronounce God's name, and, at times, unsure even of that name, or whether, in fact, God is nameable."[2] In the conclusion to his remarkable work, *Knowing God*, J. I. Packer directs our attention precisely to this disturbing yet inescapable fact. From current Christian literature, Packer notes,

> you might think that the most vital issue for any real or would-be Christian in the world today is church union, or social witness, or dialogue with other Christians and other faiths, or refuting this or that -ism, or developing a Christian philosophy and culture, or what have you. But our line of study makes the present-day concentration on these things look like a gigantic conspiracy of misdirection. Of course, it is not that; the issues themselves are real and must be dealt with in their place. But it is tragic that, in paying attention to them, so many in our day seem to have been distracted from *what was, is, and always will be the true priority for every human being—that is, learning to know God in Christ.*[3]

An Intensely Personal Experience

Much of the confusion which has resulted in the demise of the doctrine of God among evangelicals is due to a failure to know what "the knowledge of God" means. Whereas knowing God certainly entails a believing awareness that God *is*, as well as an intellectual apprehension of

1. See also Prov. 3:6; 11:9; Hosea 4:1-6; Jer. 31:33–34; Hab. 2:14; Matt. 11:27; 1 Cor. 13:12; Eph. 1:15–18; 4:11–13; Phil. 3:8–10; Col. 1:9–10; 1 John 5:20.

2. Carl F. H. Henry, *God, Revelation and Authority* (Waco: Word Books, 1982), V:9.

3. J. I. Packer, *Knowing God* (Downers Grove: InterVarsity Press, 1973), p. 254. *Emphasis mine.*

what He is *like*, this in itself does not exhaust the biblical emphasis (cf. James 2:19; Heb. 11:6). The knowledge of God which the biblical authors possessed was that sort of believing awareness and intellectual apprehension that yields an experiential oneness with God and a loving obedience to His revealed will.

Unfortunately, some have erroneously concluded that—because knowing God is more than an intellectual familiarity with facts *about* God—we may get along well enough without them. Thus, what for many passes as the knowledge of God is in fact a mindless, contentless, self-generated feeling of spiritual exultation. Indeed, on occasion I have actually heard it said that theological propositions concerning the nature of God are actually an obstacle to knowing Him in any real and lasting way. One almost gets the impression that for such people theological ignorance is heavenly bliss! But we must guard against such careless extremism lest we think that because intellectual apprehension is not sufficient for a genuine knowledge of God, it is not necessary. It is, in fact, the foundation upon which all valid Christian experience and godly fervor are built. In the absence of biblical information concerning who God is and what He is like, we may well find ourselves worshiping "foreign gods," if not a "god" fabricated from our own self-absorbed imaginations. The point of this warning is simply to emphasize that knowing God is a "both . . . and" endeavor. It is *both* thinking great thoughts about Him *and* living in such a way that those thoughts spark loving, joyful, exhilarating obedience.

Let us take but one example. The Christian who "knows" God as the providential Lord of life and history does not simply acknowledge this as an abstraction to be confessed, but a truth by which one's very heart is controlled and consumed. He or she not only studies and comprehends it as doctrine, but is enabled thereby to face each day with a calm inner assurance that a loving, all-wise Heavenly Father is in control of each momentary event. Knowing God, then, is living each day in conscious, loving dependence upon Him, wholly persuaded that the troubles and pains of life are no less His work than the blessings and victories (and glorifying His name for both!).

Thus, the truly Christian or pious mind, explains Calvin,

> recognizes God because it knows that he governs all things; and trusts that he is its guide and protector, therefore giving itself over completely to trust in him. Because it understands him to be the Author of every good, if anything oppresses, if anything is lacking, immediately it betakes itself to his protection, waiting for help from him. Because it is persuaded that he is good and merciful, it reposes in him with perfect trust, and doubts not that in his loving-kindness a remedy will be provided for all its ills. Because it acknowledges him as Lord and Father, the pious mind also deems it right and meet to observe his authority in all things, reverence his majesty, take care to advance his glory, and obey his commandments. Because it sees him to be a righteous judge, armed with severity to punish wickedness, it ever holds his judgment seat before its gaze, and through fear of him restrains itself from provoking his anger. . . . [However,] this mind restrains itself from sinning, not out of dread of punishment alone; but, because it loves and reveres God as Father, it worships and adores him as Lord. Even if there were no hell, it would still shudder at offending him alone.[4]

We see, then, that knowing God is a relational or personal experience. This is but to say that it always exists and operates within the context of commitment, trust, faith, and obedience. Religion, said Luther, is a matter of personal pronouns: *I* being able to say to God, "*my* God," and *I* knowing that God says to *me*, "*My* child." This intensely intimate and individualistic element in any true

4. John Calvin, *Institutes of the Christian Religion*, edited by John T. McNeill and translated by Ford Lewis Battles (Philadelphia: The Westminster Press, 1975), Book One, II:2.

knowledge of God is beautifully illustrated in the life of King David as reflected in Psalm 139. David's knowledge of God as omniscient (vv. 1–6), omnipresent (vv. 7–12), and omnipotent (vv. 13–18) is described not in the abstract, but in the concrete of who and what this sort of God is to him in the rigors of human experience. Donald Glenn explains:

David does not affirm that the Lord knows everything in general, that is, that He is omniscient, but that He knows everything about him personally, his thoughts and motivations (v. 2b), his words (v. 4), and his deeds (vv. 2–3). Likewise, David does not affirm that the Lord knows all things possible as well as actual, but merely that He knows all about *his* (David's) thoughts, words, and deeds long beforehand (v. 2b), and that He knew before his birth what would transpire during each of *his* days (v. 1b). Likewise, though the hypothetical structure and the use of the broadest possible cosmical and geographical merisms give an abstract quality to David's denial of escape from such knowledge (vv. 7–12), it should be emphasized that David's point is not that God is everywhere present—always and at the same time—but that everywhere he turns, *he* is confronted by the Lord who knows him so thoroughly. In addition, though David acknowledges the awesomeness of the Lord's creation in general (v. 14b), it is the Lord's intimate concern with *his* formation in his mother's womb (v. 13) that inspires his praise (v. 14). Moreover, David does not affirm that God decreed everything, but merely that He foreordained the course of *his* life (v. 16), a fact which he does not find repressive but highly precious, because he knows *he* is ever in God's thoughts (vv. 17–18). Finally, David may intimate but does not state that God will judge all men. He is, however, aware that *he* can offend Him, and is concerned that *he* walk in a way pleasing to Him (v. 24).[5]

5. Donald Glenn, "An Exegetical and Theological Exposition of Psalm 139," in *Tradition and Testament: Essays in Honor of Charles Lee Feinberg*, edited by John S. Feinberg and Paul D. Feinberg (Chicago: Moody Press, 1981), pp. 180–81.

This is not to say, Glenn is careful to note, that the statements concerning the "omni's" of God cannot be broadened "to include the fact that God is omniscient (knowing all things actual and possible), omnipresent, sovereign creator and disposer of all, and righteous judge of all men."[6] It is simply to affirm, as we did earlier, that for David these divine perfections are genuinely "known" only in the immediacy of his personal relationship to the God in whom they are manifested.

Furthermore, and somewhat paradoxically, knowing God is more than "knowing" God. It is knowing Him not in isolation but in the context of a corresponding knowledge of *ourselves*. Calvin is at his best in explaining this twofold interplay between the knowledge of God and the knowledge of ourselves. First, without the knowledge of oneself there can be no true knowledge of God:

> Each of us must . . . be so stung by the consciousness of his own unhappiness as to attain at least some knowledge of God. Thus, from the feeling of our own ignorance, vanity, poverty, infirmity, and—what is more—depravity and corruption, we recognize that the true light of wisdom, sound virtue, full abundance of every good, and purity of righteousness rest in the Lord alone. To this extent we are prompted by our own ills to contemplate the good things of God; and we cannot seriously aspire to him before we begin to become displeased with ourselves.[7]

Second, and conversely, without the knowledge of God there can be no true knowledge of ourselves:

> Again, it is certain that man never achieves a clear knowledge of himself unless he has first looked upon God's face, and then descends from contemplating him to scrutinize himself. For we always seem to ourselves righteous and

6. Ibid., p. 181.
7. Calvin, *Institutes*, Book One, I:1.

upright and wise and holy—this pride is innate in all of us—unless by clear proofs we stand convinced of our own unrighteousness, foulness, folly, and impurity. Moreover, we are not thus convinced if we look merely to ourselves and not also to the Lord, who is the sole standard by which this judgment must be measured.[8]

Again, Calvin observes that as long as we do not look beyond the earth,

being quite content with our own righteousness, wisdom, and virtue, we flatter ourselves most sweetly, and fancy ourselves all but demigods. Suppose we but once begin to raise our thoughts to God, and to ponder his nature, and how completely perfect are his righteousness, wisdom, and power—the straight-edge to which we must be shaped. Then, what masquerading earlier as righteousness was pleasing in us will soon grow filthy in its consummate wickedness. What wonderfully impressed us under the name of wisdom will stink in its very foolishness. What wore the face of power will prove itself the most miserable weakness. That is, what in us seems perfection itself corresponds ill to the purity of God.[9]

Thus Calvin concludes that man is never sufficiently "touched and affected by the awareness of his lowly state, until he has compared himself with God's majesty."[10]

We must never lose sight of the fact that this knowledge of God, in whatever degree we possess it, is always Christ-centered. That is, we only know God because of Christ as the One who reveals the Father in His incarnation. It was Jesus Himself who said: "All things have been committed to me by my Father. No one knows the Son except the Father, and no one knows the Father except the

8. Ibid., I:2.
9. Ibid.
10. Ibid., I:3.

Son and those to whom the Son chooses to reveal him"
(Matt. 11:27). Our knowledge of the Father is thus clearly
dependent on the person and work of the Son: "No one has
ever seen God, but God the only Son, who is at the Father's
side, has made him known" (John 1:18). Thus, John concludes that "the Son of God has come and has given us
understanding, so that we may know him who is true. And
we are in him who is true—even in his Son Jesus Christ. He
is the true God and eternal life" (1 John 5:20).

To the surprise of many and the discomfort of some, this
knowledge of God in and through Jesus Christ is insepara-
bly related to the practice of godliness. The apostle John is
unequivocal: "We know that we have come to know him if
we obey his commands. The man who says, 'I know him,'
but does not do what he commands is a liar, and the truth
is not in him" (1 John 2:3–4). Likewise, love of the brethren
is a product of the authentic, saving knowledge of God:
"Dear friends, let us love one another, for love comes from
God. Everyone who loves has been born of God and knows
God. Whoever does not love does not know God, because
God is love" (1 John 4:7–8). In summary we may say with
Calvin that "the knowledge of God . . . is that by which we
not only conceive that there is a God but also grasp what
befits us and is proper to his glory, in fine, what is to our
advantage to know of him. Indeed, we shall not say that,
properly speaking, God is known where there is no
religion or piety."[11]

Scripture Adds to Intuition and Cosmic Revelation

What, then, is the source of our knowledge of God?
Where or by what means may He be known?

We may first respond to this question by pointing to the
"innate" knowledge of God embedded by common grace[12]

11. Ibid., I:1.
12. For an explanation of "common grace" see chapter eight.

in the human conscience (Rom. 1:18–23; 2:14–16; and possibly John 1:9). "There is within the human mind, and indeed by natural instinct," observes Calvin, "an awareness of divinity. . . . To prevent anyone from taking refuge in the pretense of ignorance, God himself has implanted in all men a certain understanding of divine majesty."[13] That is to say, by virtue of his being in the image of God, notwithstanding the effects of Adam's transgression, man intuitively grasps the existence of deity. There is a sense, then, in which we may rightly say that atheism is a myth. The denial of God is but an attempt to suppress a knowledge which is ultimately inescapable.

There is also what we might call the "cosmic knowledge" of God, made manifest in the fashioning of the universe and the continuing government of it (Rom. 1:18–23; Acts 14:17; Psalm 19). God not only implanted in man's mind the sense of deity but also

revealed himself and daily discloses himself in the whole workmanship of the universe. As a consequence, men cannot open their eyes without being compelled to see him. Indeed, his essence is incomprehensible; hence, his divineness far escapes all human perception. But upon his individual works he has engraved unmistakable marks of his glory, so clear and so prominent that even unlettered and stupid folk cannot plead the excuse of ignorance.[14]

Although the revelation God has made of Himself by means of these two vehicles is in itself clear and undeniable, it has been corrupted and suppressed by sinful man. Consequently, though sufficient to render all without excuse before the bar of divine judgment, the revelation of God in nature and conscience does not evoke in fallen man a saving knowledge. Though the evidence is open to

13. Calvin, *Institutes*, Book One, III:1.
14. Ibid., V:1.

man, fallen man is not open to the evidence. Hence, the third and alone salvific means by which we may know God is in Scripture. Calvin observes:

> It is therefore clear that God has provided the assistance of the Word for the sake of all those to whom he has been pleased to give useful instruction because he foresaw that his likeness imprinted upon the most beautiful form of the universe would be insufficiently effective. Hence, we must strive onward by this straight path if we seriously aspire to the pure contemplation of God. We must come, I say, to the Word, where God is truly and vividly described to us from his works, while these very works are appraised not by our depraved judgment but by the rule of eternal truth.[15]

Carl Henry concurs . . .

> the way of special biblical revelation declares God himself and his revelation to be the only objective intelligible basis for statements about his nature. Only if God in fact communicates propositional information about himself, as the Judeo-Christian prophets and apostles attest, and only if that information is available to us in a trustworthy record, do we have a confident basis for expounding the divine attributes.[16]

What may have been dimly perceived in the heart and obscurely witnessed in the works of creation is now in the saving light of Scripture made gloriously clear. Herman Bavinck observes that it is to the consciousness of the believer alone, therefore, that "heaven and earth and all creatures, herbs and grass, rain and drought, fruitful and barren years, meat and drink, health and sickness, riches and poverty, yea and all things declare God. There is not

15. Ibid., VI:3.
16. Henry, *God, Revelation and Authority*, V:99.

an atom of the universe in which God's power and divinity are not revealed."[17]

The "Delightful Conviction" of Knowing God's Sovereignty

Finally, then, what is it like to know God? America's preeminent philosopher-theologian, Jonathan Edwards, has provided us with an incomparable description. It comes in the form of a poetic tribute to his bride-to-be, Sarah Pierrepont. He was eighteen and she but thirteen when it was penned:

They say [he wrote] there is a young lady in [New Haven] who is beloved of that Great Being, who made and rules the world, and that there are certain seasons in which this Great Being, in some way or other invisible, comes to her and fills her mind with exceeding sweet delight, and that she hardly cares for anything, except to meditate on him—that she expects after a while to be received up where he is, to be raised up out of the world and caught up into heaven; being assured that he loves her too well to let her remain at a distance from him always. There she is to dwell with him, and to be ravished with his love and delight forever. Therefore, if you present all the world before her, with the richest of its treasures, she disregards it and cares not for it, and is unmindful of any pain or affliction. She has a strange sweetness in her mind, and singular piety in her affections; is most just and conscientious in all her conduct; and you could not persuade her to do anything wrong or sinful, if you would give her all the world, lest she should offend this Great Being. She is of a wonderful sweetness, calmness and universal benevolence of mind; especially after this Great God has manifested

17. Herman Bavinck, *The Doctrine of God,* translated, edited and outlined by William Hendriksen (Edinburgh: The Banner of Truth Trust, 1977), p. 63.

himself to her mind. She will sometimes go about from
place to place, singing sweetly; and seems to be always full
of joy and pleasure; and no one knows for what. She loves
to be alone, walking in the fields and groves, and seems to
have some one invisible always conversing with her.[18]

This sort of intimacy with her God was equally manifest
in the man Sarah eventually wed and to whom she bore
eleven children. But with Jonathan the experience of
knowing God was early on threatened by his resistance to
the doctrine of divine sovereignty. In his pilgrimage from
initial defiance to enraptured delight in the idea of a
sovereign God we witness a marvelous illustration of what
the knowledge of God is and entails.

While in his late thirties, Edwards wrote *Personal Narrative*, a descriptive commentary on several of his more
significant religious experiences that occurred some twenty years earlier. In it we read of his struggle with the notion
of divine sovereignty:

> From my childhood up, my mind had been wont to be full
> of objections against the doctrine of God's sovereignty, in
> choosing whom he would to eternal life, and rejecting
> whom he pleased; leaving them eternally to perish, and be
> everlastingly tormented in hell. It used to appear like a
> horrible doctrine to me. But I remember the time very well,
> when I seemed to be convinced, and fully satisfied, as to
> this sovereignty of God, and his justice in thus eternally
> disposing of men, according to his sovereign pleasure.[19]

Although Edwards was not altogether certain in his own
mind how this transformation came about, of this alone he
was sure, that

18. Quoted in Ola Elizabeth Winslow, *Jonathan Edwards 1703–1758* (New York:
Octagon Books, 1973), p. 117.

19. Jonathan Edwards, *Personal Narrative*, in *Jonathan Edwards: A Profile*, ed.
David Levin (New York: Hill and Wang, 1969), p. 25.

there has been a wonderful alteration in my mind, with respect to the doctrine of God's sovereignty, from that day to this; so that I scarce ever have found so much as the rising of an objection against God's sovereignty, in the most absolute sense, in showing mercy to whom he will show mercy, and hardening and eternally damning whom he will. God's absolute sovereignty, and justice, with respect to salvation and damnation, is what my mind seems to rest assured of, as much as of any thing that I see with my eyes; at least it is so at times. But I have often times, since that first conviction, had quite another kind of sense of God's sovereignty, than I had then. I have often since, not only had a conviction, but a *delightful* conviction. The doctrine of God's sovereignty has very often appeared, an exceeding pleasant, bright and sweet doctrine to me: and absolute sovereignty is what I love to ascribe to God.[20]

Edwards proceeds to date the beginning of his fervent zeal for God (if not his conversion) from the reading of 1 Timothy 1:17: "Now to the King eternal, immortal, invisible, the only God, be honor and glory for ever and ever. Amen." As he read these words, recalled Edwards,

there came into my soul, and was as it were diffused thro' it, a sense of the glory of the Divine Being; a new sense, quite different from any thing I ever experienced before. Never any words of scripture seemed to me as these words did. I thought with myself, how excellent a being that was; and how happy I should be, if I might enjoy that God, and be wrapt up to God in Heaven, and be as it were swallowed up in Him. I kept saying, and as it were singing over these words of scripture to myself; and went to prayer, to pray to God that I might enjoy Him; and prayed in a manner quite different from what I used to do; with a new sort of affection.[21]

20. Ibid., pp. 25–26.
21. Ibid., p. 26.

This "vision" of God, if I may thusly describe it, was determinative of the whole of Edwards's life and labors. It was a knowledge of God that transformed his thoughts and stimulated his service. An entry in his *Diary* dated Saturday, January 12, 1723, captures the heightened theocentric perspective that his acquaintance with the God of Scripture produced:

> I have this day solemnly renewed my baptismal covenant and self-dedication, which I renewed when I was received into the communion of the church. I have been before God; and have given myself, all that I am and have to God, so that I am not in any respect my own: I can challenge no right in myself, I can challenge no right in this understanding, this will, these affections that are in me; neither have I any right to this body, or any of its members: no right to this tongue, these hands, nor feet: no right to these senses, these eyes, these ears, this smell or taste. I have given myself clear away, and have not retained any thing as my own. I have been to God this morning, and told Him that I gave myself *wholly* to Him. I have given every power to Him; so that for the future I will challenge no right in myself, in any respect.[22]

The attitude of many today is that this sort of delight in divine sovereignty can only cultivate a cold and secluded scholar, hemmed in by the logical rigors of a Calvinism that affords precious little appreciation for the world. But in the case of Edwards, he experienced a renewed, almost mystical, love for the created order and the majesty of God revealed therein. He wrote in *Personal Narrative* of his experience while walking in his father's pasture:

> And as I was walking there, and looked up on the sky and clouds; there came into my mind, a sweet sense of the

22. Ibid., pp. 12–13.

glorious majesty and grace of God, that I know not how to express. I seemed to see them both in a sweet conjunction: majesty and meekness join'd together: it was a sweet and gentle, and holy majesty; and also a majestic meekness; and awful sweetness; a high, and great, and holy gentleness.[23]

Everything then appeared as a channel for the divine glory:

God's excellency, his wisdom, his purity and love, seemed to appear in every thing; in the sun, moon and stars; in the clouds, and blue sky; in the grass, flowers, trees; in the water, and all nature; which used greatly to fix my mind. I often used to sit and view the moon, for a long time; and so in the day time, spent much time in viewing the clouds and sky, to behold the sweet glory of God in these things: in mean time, singing forth with a low voice, my contemplations of the Creator and Redeemer.[24]

While self, and not God, was at the center of his thoughts, Edwards was exceedingly terrified at the approach of a thunderstorm. But now, on the contrary, he tells us,

it rejoiced me. I felt God at the first appearance of a thunder-storm. And used to take the opportunity at such times to fix myself to view the clouds, and see the lightnings play, and hear the majestic and awful voice of God's thunder: which often times was exceeding entertaining, leading me to sweet contemplations of my great and glorious God. And while I viewed, used to spend my time, as it always seem'd natural to me, to sing or chant forth my meditations; to speak my thoughts in soliloquies, and speak with a singing voice.[25]

23. Ibid., p. 27.
24. Ibid., pp. 27–28.
25. Ibid., p. 28.

This, I believe, is one example of what it means to know God. Of course, Edwards's experience need not be the model after which each of us is obliged to pattern our response to the reality of who God is and what He has done. But it does set before our hearts and minds an especially vivid illustration of what knowing God can do for one's life and thought.

God Is What He Has! Or Is He?

Essence and Attribute

Anyone who takes it upon himself to enter the arena of God-talk in a meaningful and substantive way had better be prepared to joust with humility, for there is no subject which exposes the finitude of man quite like the infinitude of God! It is precisely in the vision of His power that we sense our impotence; it is in the presence of Him who is everywhere present that we come to grips with our smallness. We who constitute the nations of the earth in all our self-inflated greatness "are like a drop in a bucket," we are regarded "as dust on the scales," indeed, we are seen by Him "as worthless and less than nothing" (Isa. 40:15, 17). This God whom we seek to categorize, dissect, and discuss is "the blessed and only Ruler, the King of kings and Lord of lords, who alone is immortal and who lives in unapproachable light, whom no one has seen or can see . . ." (1 Tim. 6:15, 16). Having himself wrestled with the illimitable greatness of God's dealings with man, no less a figure than the apostle Paul was reduced to the cry:

Oh, the depth of the riches of the wisdom and knowledge
of God! How unsearchable his judgments, and his paths
beyond tracing out! Who has known the mind of the Lord?
Or who has been his counselor? Who has ever given to God,
that God should repay him? For from him and through him
and to him are all things. To him be the glory forever! Amen
(Rom. 11:33–36).

God's Autobiography

Notwithstanding the incomprehensible majesty of Deity
and the all-too-comprehensible sinful finitude of man,
God has deigned to make Himself known: "For this is what
the high and lofty One says—he who lives forever, whose
name is holy: 'I live in a high and holy place, but also with
him who is contrite and lowly in spirit, to revive the spirit
of the lowly and to revive the heart of the contrite" (Isa.
57:15). The Bible, therefore, is not simply a collection of the
inspired ruminations of humanity in its religious experience, but is in a very real sense the revelatory autobiography of God. Thus, Packer writes:

The word which God addresses directly to us is (like a royal
speech, only more so) an instrument, not only of government, but also of fellowship. For, though God is a great king,
it is not His wish to live at a distance from His subjects.
Rather the reverse: He made us with the intention that He
and we might walk together for ever in a love-relationship.
But such a relationship can only exist when the parties
involved know something of each other. God, our Maker,
knows all about us before we say anything (Ps. 139:1–4); but
we can know nothing about Him unless He tells us. Here,
therefore, is a further reason why God speaks to us: not
only to move us to do what He wants, but to enable us to
know Him so that we may love Him. Therefore God sends
His word to us in the character of both information and
invitation. It comes to woo us as well as to instruct us; it not
merely puts us in the picture of what God has done and is

doing, but also calls us into personal communion with the loving Lord Himself.[1]

The Search for Terminology

Theologians have toiled, often to despair, in the attempt to find terminology and categories whereby better to explain the nature of God. All the while acknowledging their limitations as creatures and the danger of circumscribing Him who is boundless, they have correctly noted that our knowledge of God is enhanced when we proceed according to an orderly and carefully constructed schema. Thus, various suggestions have been made as to how we may effectively classify the attributes or excellencies of God. So diligent have theologians been that it almost seems as if there are more categories for the divine attributes than there are attributes to categorize! But before we proceed any further, an attempt at defining our terms must be made.

The word *attribute* is itself somewhat unfortunate, for it suggests the notion of adding or assigning or "attributing" something to God which is not necessarily or properly His.[2] For this reason other words such as "perfections," "properties," "virtues," or—as I prefer—the "excellencies" of God, have been proposed. Whatever term we choose, it must be emphasized that God's attributes or excellencies

---

1. J. I. Packer, *Knowing God*, (Downers Grove: InterVarsity Press, 1973), p. 99.

2. An "essential" or "necessary" attribute is one that God could not lose and continue to be God. "Many of the predicates applied to God denote not attributes or essential properties of God but nonessential properties that relate God to His creatures. Relational predicates," Ronald Nash explains, "like 'creator,' 'ruler,' and 'preserver' do not denote divine attributes. A property like 'being Lord of Israel' is likewise a nonessential property. It is logically possible that God might not have had this property. He might never have created Israel, or Israel might never have accepted Yahweh as its God. Being Lord of Israel is not essential to the being of God" (*The Concept of God: An Exploration of Contemporary Difficulties with the Attributes of God* [Grand Rapids: Zondervan, 1983], p. 16).

are not something appended to His being, but together *are* His being. This introduces us to a point of dispute among theologians as to the precise relation between God's essence and His attributes.

A Perfect Living Unity

In the interests of what has been called the "simplicity" of God, theologians have been careful not to sever God's essence and attributes such that He might be thought of as a complex being. That is to say, God is not compounded of parts or a mere collection of elements, as if His attributes are but faculties or qualities pieced together to constitute a multifaceted whole. He is rather a living unity character-ized by all His perfections. The notion of God's simplicity has prompted not a few to speak of essence and attributes as in some sense identical. Herman Bavinck argued that "every attribute is identical with God's being. He *is* what he *has*."[3]

More recently, Carl Henry has echoed Bavinck's per-spective: "The divine essence is not to be differentiated from the divine attributes, but is constituted by them; the attributes define the essence more precisely."[4]

Again, Henry writes: "God's being is not the bearer of the divine attributes; rather, God's essence and attributes are identical. . . . God is, in short, the living unity of his attributes."[5] Therefore, each attribute is consistent with the others. No attribute or perfection is inferior or superior to another. All attributes are equally ultimate. God is not more holy than He is omniscient. Neither is He more loving than He is sovereign (contrary to much contemporary

3. Herman Bavinck, *The Doctrine of God,* translated, edited and outlined by William Hendriksen (Edinburgh: The Banner of Truth Trust, 1977), p. 121.
4. Carl F. H. Henry, *God, Revelation and Authority* (Waco: Word Books, 1982), V:127.
5. Ibid.

evangelical thought). Consequently, we should not exalt one attribute to the exclusion or subordination of another, but rather the one God in the unity of all His perfections.

This identity of essence and attribute, however, does not mean that the latter are but our subjective projections into God as a consequence of how we experience Him. The Lutheran Francis Pieper, like Bavinck and Henry, argued that in God essence and attribute are not separate but "absolutely identical."[6] But unlike them he appears to deny that God's attributes are objective and real. Since human reason cannot comprehend God as the infinite and absolute simplex, "God condescends to our weakness and in His Word divides Himself, as it were, into a number of attributes which our faith can grasp and to which it can cling."[7]

However, although Bavinck, Henry, and others like them insist upon an objective reality to the divine attributes, certain of their statements compromise that claim. For example, Bavinck contends that "one and the same thing is said whether it be stated that God is eternal or that he is immortal or good or just."[8] Likewise, Henry writes: "God's wisdom is his omnipotence, God's omnipotence is his justice, God's justice is his love, and so on."[9]

But if there is no genuine differentiation between the attribute of omnipotence and the attribute of justice, neither is there between God's love and His wrath. But if

6. Francis Pieper, *Christian Dogmatics* (St. Louis: Concordia, 1950), I:428.

7. Ibid.

8. Bavinck, *The Doctrine of God*, p. 121.

9. Henry, *God, Revelation and Authority*, V:132. I. A. Dorner, in a classic essay, refers to the divine simplicity as that notion to which appeal is made for proof that the "various predications about God express no objective distinctions, that none of the divine attributes is anything different from the others, that God does not simply have but *is* all his attributes. For 'that is simple, which *is* what it has.'" Dorner's essay, "Dogmatic Discussion of the Doctrine of the Immutability of God," is reprinted in *God and Incarnation in Mid-Nineteenth Century German Theology*, edited and translated by Claude Welch (New York: Oxford University Press, 1965), pp. 115–80. The above citation is on p. 120.

that be true, I have no certain assurance that what the Bible says is God's love for me is not, in fact, His wrath. It simply cannot be that God's love and wrath are identical. If they were, heaven and hell would be one and the same experience and we should have no preference for one above the other! Whereas it is true that because God loved us in Christ He caused His Son to endure that divine wrath which we deserved, that is not to say that God's love *is* His wrath. Likewise, using Henry's own example, whereas God's wisdom is compatible with His omnipotence, and His omnipotence always used wisely in the accomplishment of His purposes, wisdom and omnipotence are not identical in God's being.

It would appear, then, that out of a desire not to sever God's attributes from His essence has come a tendency to deny any genuine difference among the attributes themselves. We are, therefore, confronted with a need to avoid two extremes. On the one hand, we must not represent God as complex, as if to say His attributes are appendages of His being. They are co-ultimately the qualities or perfections which constitute what He is. On the other hand, we must not permit the simplicity of God's being to negate all distinguishable differences among the many attributes.

Would it not be preferable to say that God's attributes are the divine nature itself in its many and varied relations? For example, when the Divine Being is conceived in relation to time, He is eternal, or the attribute of eternity is manifest.[10] When the Deity is to us in our sin the source of

10. The attribute of eternality defined as divine "timelessness" has recently come under attack from several evangelical thinkers, who insist that God is not timeless but everlasting. See especially Nicholas Wolterstorff, "God Everlasting," in *God and the Good: Essays in Honor of Henry Stob*, edited by Clifton Orlebeke and Lewis Smedes (Grand Rapids: Wm. B. Eerdmans, 1975), pp. 181–203; and Stephen T. Davis, *Logic and the Nature of God* (Grand Rapids: Wm. B. Eerdmans, 1983), pp. 8–24. Ronald Nash, *The Concept of God*, while remaining uncommitted, believes Christian theism can accommodate itself to either interpretation (pp. 73–83). For a defense of divine timelessness, see Henry, *God, Revelation and Authority*, V:235–85.

unmerited salvific favor, we may say that He is gracious, or that the attribute of grace is manifest. When He is or acts in relation to space, we speak of Him as omnipresent, and so on. It would be misleading, on the other hand, to say that in His relation to space God is omnipotent, or in relation to us in our sin He is eternal. But if God's attributes are identical, this is precisely what one must say. Yet, what could these assertions possibly mean? Then, again, it may be that what Bavinck and Henry mean to say is something to the effect that it is the omnipotent, omniscient, wrathful God who loves, and it is the wise, omnipresent, jealous God who is gracious, and so on. If this be the case, no objection is forthcoming. But to say that omnipotence *is* love or that wrath *is* grace is at best confusing, at worst theologically destructive.

Having briefly considered this problem of the relation between essence and attribute, as well as the distinctions among the attributes (when properly defined), we may have here encountered precisely that limit noted earlier beyond which the finite cannot fathom the infinite. Ronald Nash has recently concluded that the notion of divine simplicity should simply be rejected as incoherent and of no practical value in deepening our understanding of the being of God.[11] This does not mean that we can no longer speak of God's essence and attributes. It is rather a sense that the discussion concerning them in their mutual relations has reached something of a theological impasse. I, for one, am not ashamed to say that I have no wholly satisfactory solution to the problem.

Classifying the Excellencies of God

Notwithstanding this confession of confusion regarding the nature of essence and attribute, we should briefly

11. Nash, *The Concept of God*, pp. 95–96.

consider the ways in which theologians have chosen to classify the excellencies of God.[12] This may best be achieved by noting three representative positions, all of which in some form or fashion overlap.

Lutheran

According to Francis Pieper, Lutherans have adopted one of two categorizations: (1) quiescent and operative attributes; or (2) negative and positive attributes. "Those who have employed the first classification define as quiescent those attributes in which no effect upon, and no relation to, the world is implied, but which are conceived as remaining within the Godhead and being apart from the world, such as eternity, simplicity, infinity."[13] On the other hand, operative attributes "is the term for all those divine attributes which denote an operation on, or a relation to, this world, such as omnipotence, omniscience, omnipresence, justice, mercy."[14] Although expressing no special preference for the second classification, Pieper chooses to treat the attributes as either negative or positive. Those who opt for this approach treat as negative such attributes as "unity, simplicity, immutability, infinity, immensity, eternity; in other words, the imperfections of creatures cannot be ascribed to God. All those attributes which are found in man, but which are ascribed to God in a higher degree or in an absolute sense are known as positive attributes, such as life, knowledge, wisdom, holiness, righteousness, truth, power, love, goodness, grace, mercy."[15]

Pieper's own list thus appears as follows:

---

12. For an extensive discussion of the methods for determining the divine attributes, again see Henry, *God, Revelation and Authority*, V:83–103.

13. Pieper, *Christian Dogmatics*, I:435.

14. Ibid.

15. Ibid.

Negative	Positive
Unity	Life
Simplicity	Knowledge
Immutability	Wisdom
Infinity	Will
Omnipresence	a) holiness
Eternity	b) justice
	c) truthfulness
	d) power
	e) goodness
	mercy
	love
	grace
	longsuffering
	patience

Arminian-Wesleyan

H. Orton Wiley[16] chooses a threefold classification: (1) the absolute attributes are those which belong to God apart from His creative work, such as spirituality, infinity, eternity, immensity, immutability, perfection; (2) the relative attributes are those arising out of the relation between Creator and creature and which require the existence of the creation itself for their manifestation. Included here are such attributes as omnipresence, omnipotence, omniscience, wisdom, goodness; and (3) the moral attributes are those which are proper to the relation between God and the moral beings under His government,

16. H. Orton Wiley, *Christian Theology* (Kansas City: Beacon Hill Press, 1940), 1:320–92.

such as holiness, love, justice, righteousness, truth, grace.

Reformed

Louis Berkhof, representative of most reformed theologians, prefers the classification of "incommunicable" and "communicable." The incommunicable attributes are those to which there is nothing analogous in the creature. The communicable attributes are those to which the properties of humanity bear some analogy (it is with reference to these attributes that man is said to be created in the image of God). Berkhof himself acknowledges that there are problems even with this approach, not least of which, as A. A. Hodge has pointed out, is that *all* God's attributes are in a certain sense communicable:

> God is infinite in his relation to space and time; we are finite in our relation to both. But he is no less infinite as to his knowledge, will, goodness, and righteousness in all their modes, and we are finite in all these respects. All God's attributes known to us, or conceivable by us, are communicable, inasmuch as they have their analogy in us, but they are all alike incommunicable, inasmuch as they are all infinite.[17]

Notwithstanding this limitation, Berkhof adopts the following list:[18]

17. A. A. Hodge, *Outlines of Theology* (London: The Banner of Truth Trust, 1972), p. 137.
18. Louis Berkhof, *Systematic Theology* (Grand Rapids: Wm. B. Eerdmans, 1972), pp. 52–81.

Incommunicable	Communicable
Self-existence	Spirituality
Immutability	Intellectual Attributes
Infinity	a) knowledge
a) perfection	b) wisdom
b) eternity	c) veracity
c) immensity	Moral Attributes
Unity	a) goodness
	general benevolence
	love
	grace
	mercy
	longsuffering
	b) holiness
	c) righteousness
	Attributes of Sovereignty
	a) sovereign will
	b) sovereign power

A more recent treatment of the divine attributes by Millard Erickson[19] is a modification upon the old natural and moral classification (found, for example, in Jonathan Edwards[20]). Erickson refers to attributes of "greatness" and attributes of "goodness."

19. Millard Erickson, *Christian Theology* (Grand Rapids: Baker Book House, 1983), I:263–300.

20. See the discussion by John Gerstner in his "Jonathan Edwards and God," *Tenth* 10 (January 1980):2–71. Of course, if "natural" means what pertains to or constitutes a nature, then all God's attributes are natural. Thus, Robert L. Dabney preferred the classification of moral and non-moral, *Lectures in Systematic Theology* (Grand Rapids: Zondervan, 1972), pp. 149–51.

Greatness	Goodness
Spirituality	Moral Purity
Personality	a) holiness
Life (self-existence)	b) righteousness
Infinity	c) justice
a) immensity/omnipresence	Integrity
b) in relation to time	a) genuineness
c) omniscience/wisdom	b) veracity
d) omnipotence	c) faithfulness
Constancy (immutability)	Love
	a) benevolence
	b) grace
	c) mercy
	d) persistence

Although my preference is for either the incommu-nicable/communicable classification of Berkhof or the greatness/goodness approach of Erickson, neither of these nor any specific mode of categorization will be used in the following discussion. My survey of the excellencies of God is simply too selective to justify a division of the attributes as we have noted them. Nevertheless, it is somewhat helpful to keep these descriptive categories in mind as we proceed.

An Indescribable Greatness

Before discussing the several attributes themselves, a word should be said concerning the technical language often employed in the subsequent pages. I certainly wish neither to frighten off the reader with unnecessarily diffi-cult terms and descriptive phrases, nor make the study of our great God a mere toilsome and abstract theological exercise. Nevertheless, God *is* great, and we are obligated, I believe, to describe Him appropriately. Carl Henry's response to those who may object to lofty language of God is directly to the point:

> If technical terms must at times . . . unavoidably intrude into our treatment of the doctrine of God, then so be it. The modern sciences, after all, abound with technical language appropriate to each field of study, and the advanced learning centers are crammed with scholars whose mastery of complex data qualifies them for the space age. Why should intelligent Christians shun a specialized grasp of the content and implications of biblical learning, and insist on only a sidewalk discussion in one-syllable words?[21]

This is not to say that a treatment of God should read like a typical insurance policy or law brief (!), but it does mean that Christians should make every effort to master those terms which best describe Him who, on occasion, will by virtue of His greatness prove indescribable!

21. Henry, *God, Revelation and Authority,* V:18.

3

One + One + One = One?

Trinitarianism

Triunity is not, properly speaking, an attribute of God. To say, for example, that God is omniscient or loving is not the same as saying that He is triune. Nevertheless, we can hardly expect to know God as we should if the doctrine of the Trinity is slighted. What has rightly been called "the primary dogma of Christianity"[1] must be given its due.

I approach this doctrine, however, with more than the usual caution. The reason is simple: there is no truth of Scripture which taxes the mind and baffles the imagination quite like the notion of triunity in God. Of course, simply stating the doctrine or giving it a definition is easy enough. But explaining in an intelligent and logically coherent way what it is that one has defined is altogether another matter. Probably the most famous definition of the doctrine of the Trinity is that of St. Augustine:

> There are the Father, the Son, and the Holy Spirit, and each is God, and at the same time all are one God; and each of

1. *One God in Trinity: An analysis of the primary dogma of Christianity,* edited by Peter Toon and James D. Spiceland (Westchester: Cornerstone Books, 1980).

them is a full substance, and at the same time all are one substance. The Father is neither the Son nor the Holy Spirit; the Son is neither the Father nor the Holy Spirit; the Holy Spirit is neither the Father nor the Son. But the Father is the Father uniquely; the Son is the Son uniquely; and the Holy Spirit is the Holy Spirit uniquely. All three have the same eternity, the same immutability, the same majesty, and the same power.[2]

Augustine has said it well; but what exactly has he said?

Self-Consistent and Compatible

In his book *The Concept of God*, Ronald Nash points to the contemporary debate concerning the coherence or consistency of the notion of God. When discussing the subject of God, observes Nash, one must be sure, first, that each individual divine attribute is self-consistent. Second, the divine attributes must be logically compatible with each other. For example, God's love and justice cannot be defined in such a way that they are mutually exclusive. In some way God must be conceived of and described as being both just and loving. Third, divine attributes must be consistent with other important concerns within a particular theological system. Finally, for theism to be coherent demands that the concept of God itself be consistent, not contradictory.[3] My reason for mentioning this is because of all we as Christians insist upon saying about God, triunity strikes many as being the least coherent, if not logically contradictory. The doctrine of the Trinity, we are told, is irrational, hardly worthy of intelligent belief. Consequently, in the minds of not a few, we are defeated before we begin. How can we expect to discuss the coherence

2. Augustine, *On Christian Doctrine*, translated by D. W. Robertson, Jr. (Indianapolis: Bobbs-Merrill, 1958), p. 10.
3. Ronald Nash, *The Concept of God* (Grand Rapids, Zondervan, 1983), pp. 12–13.

and consistency of the many attributes of the Triune God when the very notion of triunity is itself an absurdity? On any reckoning, One + One + One ≠ One!

Uniting the Three

The Christian, however, is *not* being asked to believe in such arithmetical wizardry, but only in the Bible. What, then, saith the Scripture? The Scriptures confront us with three lines of evidence, each of which is clear enough in its own right but all of which appear to pose problems when taken together.

Monotheism. That there is but one true God is an assertion at the very heart of the Judeo-Christian tradition. "Hear, O Israel: The LORD our God, the LORD is one" (Deut. 6:4). The apostle Paul is unequivocal in his monotheism: "We know that an idol is nothing at all in the world and that there is no God but one" (1 Cor. 8:4b; see also 8:5–6). Again, he insists that "there is one God and one mediator between God and men, the man Christ Jesus" (1 Tim. 2:5). See also Exod. 3:13–15; 15:11; 20:2–3; Zech. 14:9; James 2:19; Rom. 3:30. Clearly, then, we need not belabor the point. There is but one and one God only.

The Deity of Father, Son, Holy Spirit. We have a problem. There is only one God. But the Father is God. So also is the Son; likewise, the Holy Spirit. How can three be God and yet God be one? There is no escaping the fact that the biblical authors asserted both truths. Unfortunately they did not leave us with as clear an explanation as we might wish.

The deity of the Father, of course, is not disputed. No one, not even cultists (as far as I know), question the deity of Him who in Scripture is called "Father." The deity of Jesus of Nazareth and of the Holy Spirit is another matter. However, I have chosen not to develop an elaborate defense of the deity of Son and Spirit. This book is written for Christians who, I am assuming, are well acquainted with the overwhelming biblical evidence in this regard. We will proceed, therefore, on the assumption that the deity of Son and Spirit is, like that of the Father, beyond dispute.

We have thus far established that Scripture teaches these two facts: (1) there is only one God, not three; and (2) three are God—Father, Son, and Holy Spirit. The apparent contradiction in these two assertions cries out for resolution. Our third line of biblical evidence will begin to direct us to that end.

Triunity. Alongside of the biblical testimony that God is one and that three are God is the multitude of texts which in some fashion *unite* the *three* who are God, hence our term *triunity*. Since some may not be as aware of these texts which unite the three as they are of those texts which affirm the deity of each, a brief summary is in order.

Let us begin with Matthew 28:19. Our Lord says to His disciples: "Therefore go and make disciples of all nations, baptizing them in the name of the Father and of the Son and of the Holy Spirit." What is of interest here beyond the fact that Father, Son, and Holy Spirit are united in the baptismal formula is the way their unity is expressed. Jesus does not say "baptizing them in the names" (plural), but "in the name" (singular). Neither does He say "in the name of the Father, Son, and Holy Spirit," as if there were one being passing himself off under a threefold name. Rather, the definite article is repeated before each: *the* Father, and *the* Son, and *the* Holy Spirit. Thus, while Jesus distinguishes the three, with equal care he unites them under one name. This triadic formula is also found in 2 Corinthians 13:14. Paul closes this Epistle with the words: "May the grace of the Lord Jesus Christ, and the love of God, and the fellowship of the Holy Spirit be with you all." Similarly, in Ephesians 4:4–6 we read: "There is one body and one Spirit—

just as you were called to one hope when you were called—one Lord, one faith, one baptism; one God and Father of all, who is over all and through all and in all."

On numerous occasions the Father, Son, and Holy Spirit are mentioned together in unitive action or purpose relating to the life and ministry of Christ: at His conception (Luke 1:35), baptism (Matt. 3:16–17; John 1:33–34), miracles (Matt. 12:28), and ascension (Luke 24:49). There are again seemingly countless texts in which the three are in some sense one in the work of revelation and redemption. (See, for example, Acts 2:38–39; Rom. 14:17–18; 15:16, 30; 2 Cor. 1:21–22; Gal. 4:6; Eph. 2:18, 20–22; 3:14–19; Col. 1:6–8; 2 Thess. 2:13–14; Titus 3:4–6; Heb. 10:29; 1 Peter 1:2; 1 John 4:2, 13–14; Jude 20–21; Rev. 1:4–5.). The interrelationships among the Father, Son, and Holy Spirit are especially evident in the fourth Gospel, as Erickson explains,

> The Son is sent by the Father (14:24) and comes forth from him (16:28). The Spirit is given by the Father (14:16), sent from the Father (14:26), and proceeds from the Father (15:26). Yet the Son is closely involved in the coming of the Spirit: he prays for his coming (14:16); the Father sends the Spirit in the Son's name (14:26); the Son will send the Spirit from the Father (15:26); the Son must go away so that he can send the Spirit (16:7). The Spirit's ministry is understood as a continuation and elaboration of that of the Son. He will bring to remembrance what the Son has said (14:26); he will bear witness to the Son (15:26); he will declare what he hears from the Son, thus glorifying the Son (16:13–14).[4]

There it is: God is one, and three are God—triunity! None of these other lines of evidence can be dismissed or

---

4. Millard Erickson, *Christian Theology* (Grand Rapids: Baker Book House, 1983), I:331–32.

subordinated to either of the other two. The task of the early church, and our task as well, is to construct an explanation which best accounts for all three verities.

Unity of Essence, Trinity of Personhood

To simplify matters, let us consider what I believe are the only three possible solutions to the problem.

The first alternative is to stress the unity of the one God to the exclusion of the full and co-equal deity of Father, Son, and Holy Spirit. That is to say, the first line of biblical evidence noted above is given prominence. The doctrinal construct that results has been called "Monarchianism." Historically, monarchians have opted for one of two explanations concerning the Son and Holy Spirit. Dynamic monarchianism conceives of Jesus prior to His baptism as wholly human. As a reward for His exceptional moral virtue, Jesus was "adopted" as God's Son and empowered by the spirit (note well: "spirit," not "Spirit"), through which (not "whom") He subsequently performed His many miracles. Thus, Jesus was "divine" by virtue of a received power, not because of any supposed equality of nature with the Father.

Whereas dynamic monarchianism or adoptionism did not flourish in the early centuries of Christian history, its sister view did. Modalistic monarchianism, as it is called, was driven by a twin conviction: the oneness of God, and the full deity of Christ. The only viable way to maintain both, so they thought, was to identify the Son with the Father (and the Spirit likewise). Thus, they posited one God who could be designated as Father, Son, or Holy Spirit, depending upon the emphasis desired or the activity in view (be it creative, redemptive, or revelatory, respectively). These names did not stand for real and objective personal distinctions in the Godhead, but simply were different expressions for the same God. Consequently, Jesus was conceived to be but one of three successive forms or "modes" whereby the one God manifested Himself. Father, Son, and Holy Spirit are verbal descriptions only of three different phases under which the one Divine Being reveals itself.

Let me illustrate. While in elementary school I was called, under differing circumstances, by all three of my names. Schoolteachers insisted upon calling me by my first name, *Charles*. My parents and sister used my middle name, *Sam*, whereas my friends, (as was the custom in those days) simply called me *Storms*. Thus, the *one* young boy, depending upon the circumstances and relationships, was referred to (now) as Charles when a student, (then) Sam when a son, and (again) Storms when a friend. But I was still only *one person*. Such, by way of analogy, was the answer of modalistic monarchians to the evidence of Scripture concerning the one God who is Father, Son, and Holy Spirit. The Father was God as Creator, the Son was God as Redeemer, and the Holy Spirit was God as Revealer and Sanctifier. Clearly, however, this scheme does not do full justice to the biblical witness concerning the personal distinctions in the Godhead and the multifaceted interrelationships among Father, Son, and Holy Spirit (see especially the emphasis in the Gospel of John noted earlier).

The second alternative to our problem has never had many advocates. Whereas the first option emphasized the oneness of God to the exclusion of an objective and distinctive reality to Father, Son, and Holy Spirit, the second possibility was to stress the full deity of Father, Son, and Spirit such that any sense of unity was obscured (at most, a unity of purpose or will was retained). The result is "tritheism," the existence of three independent gods. This form of polytheism is simply not a viable option for anyone who takes the Bible seriously.

The third and, I believe, only legitimate alternative is to accept without diminution both the oneness of God and the full deity of Father, Son, and Spirit. Full recognition is given to those texts which emphasize in some sense the unified relation in being and activity among those who are yet in another sense distinct. Again, historically the church has used this formula:

God is one in *essence (ousia)*

God is three in *person (prosōpon)*

Thus, historic trinitarianism does not assert that God is one and three in the same sense, but rather: *that* in respect to which God is one is "essence," and *that* in respect to which God is three is "person." In affirming triunity in God, we are saying that God is one in a sense different from the sense in which He is three. Stephen Davis illustrates it as follows:

> Joseph, Mary and Jesus are separate things and Joseph, Mary and Jesus are one thing. This sentence seems inconsistent until we realize that the sort of thing referred to in the first conjunct is a person and that the sort of thing referred to in the second is a family.[5]

We may thus speak about Father, Son, and Holy Spirit both in terms of what is common to all (essence) and what is proper to each (person). When we refer to what is proper to each (person), we may rightly say that the Father ≠ the Son or the Holy Spirit, the Son ≠ the Father or the Holy Spirit, and the Holy Spirit ≠ the Father or the Son. When we refer to what is common to all (essence), we may rightly say that the Father = God; the Son = God; and the Holy Spirit = God. Therefore, the Father, Son, and Holy Spirit together = God.

To put it yet another way, that which constitutes the Father as Father and not Son or Spirit is proper to Him alone, namely, *paternity* and all that it implies. That which

5. Stephen T. Davis, *Logic and the Nature of God* (Wm. B. Eerdmans, 1983), p. 135.

constitutes the Son as Son and not Father or Spirit is proper to Him alone, namely, *sonship* and all that it implies. Likewise, that which constitutes the Spirit as Spirit and not Father or Son is proper to Him alone, namely, *spiration* (or *procession*). But that in respect to which the Father is *God* is likewise true of the Son and Spirit; and that in respect to which the Son is *God* is likewise true of the Father and Spirit; and, again, that in respect to which the Spirit is *God* is likewise true of the Father and Son.

In addition, it is important to remember that the trinitarian relationships which we refer to as paternity, sonship, and procession are meaningful only in respect to the *personal distinctions* in the Godhead, and not the divine essence itself. That is to say:

(1) The Father generates the Son *as Son*, but *not* the Son *as God*. The Son derives "sonship" from the Father, but not deity. In respect to deity, the Son is God in Himself (*autotheos*).

(2) The Father and Son are They from whom the Spirit proceeds *as Spirit*, but *not* the Spirit *as God*. The Spirit derives "spirituality" (for lack of a better term) from the Father and Son, but not deity. In respect to deity, the Spirit is God in Himself (*autotheos*).

On this basis, an earlier form of the Nicene Creed was not incorrect in saying that the Son (and, by application, the Spirit also) is "God of God." The Son is "God of God" with respect to the personal relationship between Father and Son. The Father *as Father* is the principium (He by whom the Son is begotten) of the Son *as Son*, but not the source or principium of the Son *as God*. The Son is God of Himself and not of another. Likewise, the Holy Spirit is "God of God" with respect to the personal relationship between Spirit and Father and between Spirit and Son. The Father *as Father* is the principium (source, or He from whom the Spirit proceeds) of the Holy Spirit *as Holy Spirit*, but not the source or principium of the Holy Spirit *as God.* Again, the Son *as Son* is the principium (source, or He from whom the Spirit proceeds)[6], of the Holy Spirit *as Holy Spirit,* but not the source or principium of the Holy Spirit *as God.* The Holy Spirit is God of Himself and not of another.

This explanation may be summarized in the following way:

Father	—is	God from whom God exists
	—is not	God from God
Son	—is	God from God
	—is	God from whom God exists
Holy Spirit	—is	God from God
	—is not	God from whom God exists

Or, to put it yet another way:

The Father begets the Son and is He from whom the Holy Spirit proceeds, but the Father is neither begotten nor does He proceed.

The Son is begotten of the Father and is He from whom the Holy Spirit proceeds, but He neither begets nor proceeds.

The Holy Spirit proceeds from both the Father and the Son, but He neither begets nor is He one from whom another proceeds.

As someone perceptively said of the doctrine of the Trinity: "Try to explain it, and you'll lose your mind; But try to deny it, and you'll lose your soul!"

6. For a discussion of the "Filioque," i.e., the doctrine that the Spirit proceeds from the Son as well as from the Father, see Alasdair Heron, "The *Filioque* Clause," in *One God in Trinity*, pp. 62–77.

The Search for Analogies

As you were forewarned, there is *indeed* no doctrine which taxes the mind and baffles the imagination quite like the notion of triunity in God. The explanation I have put forth is not new. It is simply a cumulative expression of what I believe are the best efforts by Christian thinkers over the past 1,900 years as they wrestled with the three lines of biblical evidence discussed earlier.

But are there not illustrations or analogies in man and nature whereby to make this doctrine more intelligible? Many have tried. For example, Bavinck points to:

> the three dimensions of space; the three measurements of time; the three kingdoms of nature: matter, spirit, and the union of the two in man; the solid, fluid, and gaseous state; the power of attraction, repulsion, and equilibrium; the three functions of the human soul: reasoning, feeling, and desiring; the three capacities of the soul: mind, will, and moral nature; the three factors that constitute a family: husband, wife and child; the three classes in society: teachers, soldiery, and peasantry . . . the three tones in music: key-tone, tierce-tone, and quint-tone; the rainbow and its many colors; the sun with its quickening, illumining, and warming energy; the three basis colors: yellow, red, and blue, etc.[7]

One of the more popular illustrations was articulated by Augustine. He pointed to the nature of love: the lover, the object loved, and the love which unites them. In the final analysis, however, each and every illustration fails.

This does not mean that the doctrine is irrational or even illogical. "Trinitarianism," Carl Henry reminds us, "does not require belief in rational contradiction; if it did,

7. Herman Bavinck, *The Doctrine of God*, translated, edited and outlined by William Hendriksen (Edinburgh: The Banner of Truth Trust, 1977), p. 323.

neither sound Christian faith nor reason could commend it."[8] What we are saying is that there is a sense in which God is one (essence) and a sense in which He is three (person). The one God exists eternally in three distinct but not independent persons: Father, Son, and Holy Spirit. Roger Nicole writes, "These three are fully equal in every divine perfection. They possess alike the fullness of the divine essence."[9] Obviously, this explanation is only as good as the terms we have employed. "Essence" and "person" may not be susceptible of a definition that will fully resolve all problems or convince all skeptics. But they have served the church well for these many centuries and are, in my opinion, the best available explanatory model by which to deal with the evidence the Bible presents. It also enables us to avoid a logical contradiction. A contradictory statement is one in which we assert that "A is non-A at the same time and in the same respect." But the way in which God is said to be one (namely, in essence) is not the same in time, or respect with the way in which God is said to be three (namely, in person).

The doctrine of the Trinity, therefore, is neither contradictory not inconsistent with Scripture. It is logically coherent and the best available explanation of the biblical data. That it remains a mystery in that we cannot and (on this side of heaven) may never *fully* understand it is no cause for despair. Rather, we should in our own way share in the experience of Isaiah the prophet and respond even as he:

8. Carl F. H. Henry, *God, Revelation and Authority* (Waco: Word Books, 1982), V:167. A more recent debate on the logical status of the doctrine of the Trinity may be found in John V. Dahms, "How Reliable Is Logic?" *JETS* 21 (December 1978):369–80; Norman Geisler, "'Avoid Contradictions' (I Tim. 6:20): A Reply to John Dahms," *JETS* 22 (March 1979):55–65; John Dahms, "A Trinitarian Epistemology Defended: A Rejoinder to Norman Geisler," *JETS* 22 (June 1979):133–48; and Norman Geisler, "Avoid *All* Contradictions: A Surrejoinder to John Dahms," *JETS* 22 (June 1979):149–59.

9. Roger Nicole, "The Meaning of the Trinity," in *One God in Trinity*, p. 2.

In the year that King Uzziah died, I saw the Lord seated on
a throne, high and exalted, and the train of his robe filled
the temple. Above him were seraphs, each with six wings:
With two wings they covered their faces, with two they
covered their feet, and with two they were flying. And they
were calling to one another: "Holy, holy, holy is the Lord
Almighty; the whole earth is full of his glory." At the sound
of their voices the doorposts and thresholds shook and the
temple was filled with smoke. "Woe to me!" I cried. "I am
ruined! For I am a man of unclean lips, and I live among a
people of unclean lips, and my eyes have seen the King, the
Lord Almighty" (Isa. 6:1–5.)

His Eye Is on the Sparrow

Omniscience

D ivine omniscience," says Ronald Nash, "means that God holds no false beliefs. Not only are all of God's beliefs true, the range of his knowledge is total; He knows all true propositions."[1] Simply put: God's knowledge is infinite. "Great is our LORD and mighty in power; his understanding has no limit" (Ps. 147:5).

In discussing the knowledge of God, a distinction is often made between the "knowledge of vision" and the "knowledge of intelligence." The knowledge of vision is what God has of Himself as well as all things that either were, are, or shall be at some point in time—i.e., of all things He has decreed to be, even though they do not as yet exist. The knowledge of intelligence, on the other hand, is not of things that are or shall be by any decree of God, but of such things as *could be* by the power and decree of God if He were of a mind so to act—i.e., of things which could be but will not be. The distinction, then, is this: God knows all things He *could* do, if He so willed (knowledge of intelligence), as well as all things He *has done*, having already decreed that they should occur (knowledge of

---

1. Ronald Nash, *The Concept of God* (Grand Rapids: Zondervan, 1983), p. 51.

vision). Thus, A. H. Strong defines divine omniscience as "God's perfect and eternal knowledge of all things which are objects of knowledge, whether they be actual or possible, past, present or future."[2]

Innate, Instant, and Independent Infallibility

One way in which the nature of God's knowledge may be better expressed and explained is by placing it in a series of contrasts with what we know to be true of our own cognitive abilities.

We begin by noting that God's knowledge is intuitive, not discursive. Our knowledge is discursive in that it comes by way of observation, reasoning, comparison, induction, deduction, and so on. In other words, we *learn*. But God's knowledge is intuitive, by which is meant that it is innate and immediate. God does not learn; He knows, and that in one simple, all-comprehensive act.

Traditionally, theologians have also contrasted God's knowledge with ours by saying that His knowledge is simultaneous, not successive. He sees things at once and in their totality, whereas we know only as the objects of knowledge are brought before us, one bit after another. With God, however, the act of perception is complete and instantaneous. Simply put: God thinks about all things at once (all things, that is, which from our perspective are either past, present, or future). Those who contend for this characteristic of the divine knowledge insist that as a result God has neither memory nor foreknowledge. Memory, explains Shedd,

> can belong only to the finite mind. As there is nothing past in the consciousness of God, there can be no such act in him as that of recalling the past to mind. He neither remembers nor forgets, in the literal sense, because the

2. A. H. Strong, *Systematic Theology* (Old Tappan: Fleming H. Revell, 1970), p. 282.

whole of his knowledge is simultaneously and perpetually present. And this whole, or sum total, of omniscience, includes all that which for the creature is included in past, present, and future time.[3]

Likewise, it is not entirely accurate to speak of God as having foreknowledge. Just as there is nothing past in the consciousness of God, there is nothing future in the consciousness of God. The word *foreknowledge* is simply a way of expressing the nature and extent of God's knowledge from the vantage point of men on earth—in time. We assert that God knows what we will do *before* we do it, hence He has *fore*knowledge. But from God's perspective there is neither "before" nor "after." God apprehends and knows all things (things which from our point of view may be past, present, or future) in one simultaneous act of cognition. All things past, present, or future are ever before Him at once, not in the sense that temporal events lose their order of progression for us, but in the sense that God's *knowledge* of them is without chronological sequence.

Were it at all possible to do so, I would quietly skip over the question of God's relation to time. I must confess from the outset that I find the subject to be as difficult as any in theology, and on occasion more than my fragile mind is competent to conceive. Philosophers are today debating the issue with ever-increasing fervor and are themselves far from a consensus.[4] My purpose in this book would not be served by attempting to engage them in dialogue, even if I were philosophically capable of doing so (which I am not). My immediate concern is simply to determine as best I can the propriety of using the word *"fore*knowledge" with respect to God. I am not a professional philosopher

3. William G. T. Shedd, *Dogmatic Theology* (Minneapolis: Klock & Klock Christian Publishers, 1979), I:348–49.
4. See note 10, chapter two.

and therefore feel a bit uneasy taking up this question. I am even more uneasy about some of the conclusions (extremely tentative) to which the subsequent arguments have led me. However, these doubts and fears notwithstanding, the subject must be broached (albeit briefly).

As I remarked earlier, whereas all biblical theists affirm that God is "eternal," there is a difference of opinion as to how the notion of eternality is to be defined. Most reformed theologians since the time of the Reformation have understood the eternity of God as entailing His "timelessness." A number of more contemporary thinkers prefer the word *everlasting* and insist that temporal predicates such as "past" and "future" may indeed be used in our discussion of God (and not just figuratively). We begin our inquiry with the doctrine of timelessness.

What exactly is meant in saying that God is "timelessly" eternal? The fundamental notion seems to be that God exists outside the temporal sequence altogether. Consequently, Dabney explains, the "past and the future are as distinctively and immutably present with the Divine Mind, as the present."[5] God transcends time and thus both exists and thinks in a "perpetual or eternal now." Time, with its past, present, and future, is a creaturely limitation to which God is not subject. God knows, for example, that in *our* experience the events of January 1 precede, and those of January 3 follow, the events of January 2. But in God's mind the events of January 1, 2, and 3 are known simultaneously. None of the events of the first, second, and third days of January is anything other than "present" to God.[6]

5. Robert L. Dabney, *Lectures in Systematic Theology* (Grand Rapids: Zondervan, 1972), p. 152.
6. Similar definitions of divine timelessness may be found in Millard Erickson, *Christian Theology* (Grand Rapids: Baker Book House, 1983), I:274; A. H. Strong, *Systematic Theology*, p. 276; A. A. Hodge, *Outlines of Theology* (London: The Banner of Truth Trust, 1972), p. 143; Louis Berkhof, *Systematic Theology* (Grand Rapids: Wm. B. Eerdmans, 1972), p. 60; and Francis Pieper, *Christian Dogmatics* (St. Louis: Concordia, 1950), I:446.

The difficulty of this doctrine is acknowledged even by those who affirm it. Shedd says it is a greater mystery than the Trinity[7], and Berkhof believes that it is perhaps "incapable of solution in our present condition."[8] I also have difficulty with the idea of divine timelessness; indeed, I am not at all sure what this doctrine is saying about God. Many of the statements made in connection with the notion of timelessness sound impressive enough, but I must confess they do not at all times make sense. This discussion, therefore, is going to get a bit involved, but bear with me for just a moment.

All acknowledge that from our vantage point as finite creatures, events are either past, present, or future. The traditional concept of timelessness, if I understand it correctly, insists that past and future are not applicable to God: all is present. Charles Hodge says that with God "there is no distinction between the present, past, and future; but all things are equally and always present to Him."[9] Shedd is even more explicit. To the divine consciousness, he argues, "the creation of the world is not in the past, and the destruction of the world is not in the future."[10] Notwithstanding my respect for Hodge, Shedd, and others like them, these statements appear to me quite baffling. I simply do not understand how it can be said, for example, that the second coming of Christ is *present* in the consciousness of God. Let me develop this point a bit further.

God *now* knows infallibly that Christ *will* return, but does not now know Christ *as* returning, because Christ *now* is not returning. In other words, God *now* knows (infallibly, exhaustively, immutably) *as future* the return of

7. Shedd, *Dogmatic Theology*, 1:350.

8. Berkhof, *Systematic Theology*, p. 60.

9. Charles Hodge, *Systematic Theology* (Grand Rapids: Wm. B. Eerdmans, 1970), 1:385.

10. Shedd, *Dogmatic Theology*, 1:346.

Christ. However, He does not *now* know *as present* the
return of Christ, because the return of Christ is not a
presently occurring event. When the future return of
Christ finally comes to pass, God will at the time of its
occurrence know it *as an occurring* or present event. After
it has occurred, He will know it *as an already-occurred* or
past event. But at present, *now* (the redundancy is for
emphasis), God can know Christ's return as *neither* present *nor* past, because it is still future. To say that God *now*
knows Christ's return as present is to say that God *now*
exists *in the future*. Of course, in the future God *will be
existing* (and will forever continue to exist, even as in the
past He never "not existed," if I may phrase it thusly). But
what could it possibly mean to say that *now* God exists in
the future? God does not *now* exist in the future, because
the future is by definition subsequent to any *now*. It
appears to me incoherent to say that there already exists a
being at a time which, by definition, has not yet been. How
can God *now* exist *later?* But the traditional timeless
doctrine must assert that God does now exist later, or the
notion that the future is present to His consciousness will
have to be abandoned (or we will have to redefine our
terms, "past," "present," and "future"). My understanding
is that the future is present to God only in the sense that it
has already been ordained by God and exists in His mind
as a "thing" that *will* exist in actuality, but does *not now*
exist in actuality.

Now this may well be what Hodge, Shedd, and others
mean by the doctrine of divine timelessness (to wit, that all
is present to God because infallibly foreordained by Him).
If that is the case, I certainly have no quarrel with them or
it. But for the sake of argument, let us assume that it is not.
I would then expect the proponent of the timeless doctrine to respond by saying that my entire preceding
discussion is senseless because the terms "past" and
"future" are not applicable to God. But that is begging the
question. I want to know *why* they are not applicable to

God, and it will not do simply to assert that it is because He is timeless! It seems to me that in some sense these terms *must* be applicable to Him.

Let me put the question this way.

(1) Did God exist before the world did? Of course He did. The world is not eternal. There was a "time," if you will, when the only existent thing was God. Or, again, the world, but not God, began to be (cf. Ps. 90:1–2).

(2) Did God create the world? Of course He did. No one who takes the Bible seriously denies that God created all things.

(3) *If* God existed *before* the world (that is, if once God existed and the world did not), and *if* God created it, then *prior* to God's creation of the world the world's existence was *future* to God. Otherwise the world is eternally exist-ent. It seems to me inescapable that "future" *is* a word applicable to God in His relation to events and things. Again, how can we possibly say that God causes what is nonexistent to become existent (the world) and yet sus-tains no temporal relation to it?

Suppose, for the sake of argument, that God has already chosen to annihilate some material object, such as a rock or a book, at some point in *our* future. I am not saying that He did (or will), but surely it is logically possible for Him to have done so (and to do so). It is true, is it not, that once God *has* annihilated the rock, that is, caused its nonexist-ence, the *existence* of the rock is *past* vis-á-vis God? One cannot say its existence is present in relation to God because it does not presently exist. But we can say, I believe, that God *now* knows the *past* existence of the rock in the sense that He has exhaustive and infallible *memory* of it. That is, God *now* knows everything about and associated with the rock when it used to exist. I see no problem, therefore (that does not mean there is none!), in asserting both that the existence of the rock was at one time still *future* to God, because not yet existent, and is now *past* to God, because no longer existent.

I readily concede that all the events of time, be they past, present, or future, are as thoroughly known by God now *as if* they were actually existent. But if they are not actually existent, then their actual existence is either already past or still future to God, even though His knowledge of them *now* (as past or future) is exhaustive, infallible, and immutable.

My predication of the terms "past" and "future" to God is not without its problems. For example, an objection from the traditional perspective is that it means what is true of God today was not true of Him yesterday and will not be true of Him tomorrow: hence, God is not immutable. That is to say, if God's knowledge changes (what is today known by God only as future will tomorrow be known by God as present), God Himself changes. Indeed, according to this objection, it may be said that unless God is timeless, He learns.

I do not think this objection is valid (but it is, admittedly, the most difficult to answer). The only thing not true of God today that will be true of Him tomorrow is that tomorrow He will know *as present* what today He knows *as future*. But the extent and nature of the content of His knowledge are constant. His knowledge of the event when it is present will not then be better or more complete than His knowledge of the event while it was yet future.

Surely if God has foreordained future event "X" (as I believe He has foreordained *all* events), there is *nothing*, no thought, feeling, circumstance, antecedent or consequent, in any conceivable relation to "X," which God does not *now* know exhaustively and infallibly. The only difference in God (if it may rightly be called a "difference") is that when "X" finally occurs, it (and all its concomitants) will be present to God rather than future. But God's knowledge of "X" will have changed *only* if we *deny* that God ordained "X" and its related circumstances. The problem we have in conceiving of this is because no matter how thoroughly we as humans think we know what a future event will be like, when it finally occurs we learn or experience something which before its occurrence we could neither anticipate nor understand. But that is because we did not infallibly and immutably ordain the event. Our present knowledge of the event was necessarily limited by the fact that it could, and most likely did, turn out slightly different from what we expected. But this is altogether impossible in the case of a sovereign, omniscient, foreordaining God by whom all future events have been decreed and thus perfectly known in advance of their occurrence.

Why do we assume that God cannot *now* know a future event just as exhaustively and infallibly as He *will* know it once it occurs? The assumption is valid, as I noted, only if one denies that the future event was in every conceivable respect and relation ordained/decreed by God.

Someone may still object that it simply is not the same thing *now* to know a future event, even exhaustively, and *then* to know it when it occurs. The actual experience of being present witness to the event when it occurs adds something to the knower that was absent when the event was known only as future, even though certainly known. This objection, however, holds true only for finite creatures. It need not, and in my opinion does not, hold true for an infinite, omniscient, sovereign God. If God knows Himself and all ordained events exhaustively and infallibly, then there is nothing in any conceivable relation to those events—even His own "experience" of them—which God does not *now* know as thoroughly as He *will* know when they occur. One may still wish to contend that even God's exhaustive and infallible knowledge *now* of a future event He has ordained/decreed is *not* identical with and therefore no substitute for what will be true of God when the event finally occurs. Although I do not accept this objection, and for reasons already stated, I think the discussion of this aspect of our problem has gone far enough. And if, after all this, one still thinks God's knowledge, and therefore God, has changed, then so be it. But such "change" as this is no threat to the biblical doctrine of omniscience and immutability as I understand them.

Of course, the defender of the timeless doctrine will not stop here. He will proceed to point out that it is not simply because of a perceived threat to omniscience and immutability that he defends the doctrine, but because he believes it is in the Bible. (The texts normally referred to as proof of divine timelessness are Gen. 21:33; Ps. 90:1–4; 102:12, 25–27; Isa. 41:4; 44:6; 57:15; John 8:58; 1 Tim. 1:17; 6:16; 2 Peter 3:8; Jude 25; Rev. 1:8; 21:6; 22:13). But most of the pertinent texts, if not all, need teach no more than that God is "everlastingly" eternal, that is, without beginning or end. I say "most" of them because a few of them are problematic:

> But do not forget this one thing, dear friends: With the Lord a day is like a thousand years, and a thousand years are like a day. (2 Peter 3:8).
> "I tell you the truth," Jesus answered, "before Abraham was born, I am!" (John 8:58).

And in the context of Psalm 90, the eternality of God is contrasted with the transience of human life. God is everlasting: "Before the mountains were born or you brought forth the earth and the world, from everlasting to everlasting you are God" (v. 2).

As over against man, who is of dust and to dust must return, God is without beginning or end. Clearly the psalmist is telling us that because of this difference a millennium is not from the divine perspective what it is from the human perspective. One thousand years is in the sight of God what yesterday is to us—gone before we know it. It is from God's perspective what a nightwatch (four hours) is in ours. Similarly, Peter rebuts the scoffers with the fact that what may to them appear as an interminable delay is but a day in the divine purpose. Richard Bauckham observes that although "the period until the End may seem long by human standards, in God's sight it passes rapidly."[11] But this does not mean, argues Bauckham, that God's eternity is to be construed as atemporality. Rather, the point is that "God's perspective on time is not limited by a human life span. He surveys the whole of history and sets the times of events in accordance with his agelong purpose. His perspective is so much more comprehensive than that of men and women who, accustomed to short-term expectations, are impatient to see the Parousia in their own lifetime."[12]

But unfortunately this does not explain *why* God's perspective on time is more comprehensive than man's. Is it because God has a perfect and exhaustive knowledge of the Parousia and all the preceding events of human history, having ordained them? Or is it because the from-our-perspective future coming of Christ is in some sense *present* to God, as the proponents of divine timelessness have insisted? At this time I simply do not know.

But what about John 8:58? The contrast is explicit: of Abraham it may be said, he "was born" (or, "came into existence," *genesthai*). But of Himself Jesus says, "I am" *(egō eimi)*. Jesus does not say, "before Abraham was born, *I was*," but *"I am."* Therefore, advocates of divine timelessness see here a reference not merely to Christ's preexistence but to His transcedence above time altogether. C. H. Dodd comments:

11. Richard J. Bauckham, *Word Biblical Commentary. Jude, 2 Peter* (Waco: Word Books, 1983), p. 309.
    12. Ibid.

The implication is that Jesus does not stand within the temporal series of great men, beginning with Abraham and continuing through the succession of the prophets, so as to be compared with them. His claim is not that He is the greatest of the prophets, or even greater than Abraham himself. He belongs to a different order of being. The verb *genesthai* is not applicable to the Son of God at all. He stands outside the range of temporal relations.[13]

Likewise, G. C. Berkouwer insists that Jesus "is not subject to calendar dates but reaches infinitely higher, reaches into the depths of eternity."[14] The statement "breaks through the categories of time-bound thinking which imagines it can interpret Christ in terms of our existence."[15]

Whereas this statement of our Lord is certainly compatible with the doctrine of divine timelessness, it does not require it. It may again simply be a reference to Christ as eternally everlasting, without beginning (unlike Abraham) or end. Whereas Abraham at a point in time began to be, the pre-incarnate second person of the Trinity simply *is*. His life, unlike that of Abraham, never began. Furthermore, the use of the phrase "I am" may be due more to the influence of Exodus 3:14 (a dominant Christological theme in John's Gospel; cf. also Deut. 32:39; Isa. 41:4; 43:10; 46:4) than to a conscious attempt to claim timelessness. In summary, I find this text and 2 Peter 3:8 to be compatible with *either* view of God's eternity. The issue, therefore, will have to be decided on other grounds (or texts).

I must again stress that I am not in any sense certain of these arguments. God may well be "timeless" as traditionally defined. However, at this stage in my thinking the notion of "eternally everlasting" appears more cogent. But

13. C. H. Dodd, *The Interpretation of the Fourth Gospel* (Cambridge: University Press, 1970), p. 261.

14. G. C. Berkouwer, *The Person of Christ* (Grand Rapids: Wm. B. Eerdmans, 1973), p. 166.

15. Ibid.

on *either* position, be it noted, God's knowledge is infinite and immutable. *What* God knows and *how well* He knows it are neither reduced nor enhanced by His relation to time. What His relation to time causes us to do is ask whether *fore*knowledge is anthropopathic (figurative) or literal.

In questioning the coherence of divine timelessness, I wish to distance myself from some of the reasons why other contemporary thinkers have done so. Clark Pinnock[16] rejects timelessness because he believes that—if true—it would destroy the genuine contingency of future events. But, as I have already remarked, rejection of divine time-lessness does *not* threaten the sovereignty of God. A denial of timelessness does *not* entail an affirmation of the contingency of future events (more on this below). Again, Nicholas Wolterstorff[17] rejects divine timelessness because he believes it entails divine immutability, which he rejects. However, as will be made clear in chapter seven, I believe immutably in divine immutability! Consequently, the doc-trines of divine immutability and God's sovereign decree of all future events are not dependent on the notion of timelessness. One may, I believe, reject the latter and affirm the former.

In conclusion, I think it *is* proper or literal, not anthro-popathic, to speak of *fore*knowledge in God. But should I later be proven wrong, it will neither disturb me nor adversely affect my view of divine omniscience or the certainty of God-known and God-ordained events.

Before engaging in this extended parenthetical discus-sion, I was describing the ways in which God's knowledge may be contrasted with ours. Returning now to that theme, we observe that God's knowledge is independent, not

16. Clark Pinnock, "The Need for a Scriptural, and Therefore a Neo-Classical Theism," in *Perspectives on Evangelical Theology*, edited by Kenneth S. Kantzer and Stanley N. Gundry (Grand Rapids: Baker Book House, 1979), p. 40.

17. Nicholas Wolterstorff, "God Everlasting," in *God and the Good: Essays in Honor of Henry Stob*, edited by Clifton Orlebeke and Lewis Smedes (Grand Rapids: Wm. B. Eerdmans, 1975), pp. 181–203.

dependent. He does not receive His knowledge from anyone outside Himself: "Who has understood the Spirit of the LORD, or instructed him as his counselor? Whom did the LORD consult to enlighten him, and who taught him the right way? Who was it that taught him knowledge or showed him the path of understanding?" (Isa. 40:13–14).

As we have already alluded to in the discussion of God's foreknowledge, His knowledge is infallible, not subject to mistake. God is *always* correct in what He knows. God's knowledge is also immutable, not subject to change. He cannot change in what He knows, by either increase or decrease. He neither discovers nor forgets.

Finally, God's knowledge is infinite, not partial, and that in several important respects. First, as Carl Henry explains:

> God thoroughly knows himself; in the divine nature there are no dark and hidden recesses. God also thoroughly knows his created universe. "Known unto God are all his works from the beginning of the world" (Acts 15:18). He comprehensively knows both his inanimate creation (Ps. 147:4) and also the creaturely world (Matt. 10:29). No aspect of our vast universe, which some space-age observers are prone to consider infinite, is concealed from God.[18]

Second, God knows our inner man thoroughly and exhaustively. No secret of the human heart, no thought of the mind, escapes His gaze. Henry writes: "Psychologists and psychoanalysts speak of deep areas of subconscious experience of which human beings are hardly aware. But God knows all men thoroughgoingly, psychologists and psychoanalysts and theologians included."[19]

In Psalm 139 David says that God's knowledge of him encompasses the whole of life: "You know when I sit and when I rise; you perceive my thoughts from afar. You

---

18. Carl F. H. Henry, *God, Revelation and Authority* (Waco: Word Books, 1982), V:268.
19. Ibid.

discern my going out and my lying down; you are familiar with all my ways" (Ps. 139:2–3). Donald Glenn explains that David employs a figure of speech called merism, "in which polar opposites are used to indicate the totality of all generically related acts, events, localities, and so on."[20] My most common and casual acts, my most insignificant and trivial movements, none escape thine eye! Every emotion, feeling, idea, resolve, aim, doubt, fear or anxious moment is like an open book to your penetrating gaze. And all this from afar! The distance between heaven and earth by which men vainly imagine God's knowledge to be circumscribed offers no obstacle. In Charles Spurgeon's interpretation:

> Though my thought be invisible to the sight, though as yet I be not myself cognizant of the shape it is assuming, yet thou hast it under thy consideration, and thou perceivest its nature, its source, its drift, its result. Never dost thou misjudge or wrongly interpret me: my inmost thouught is perfectly understood by thine impartial mind. Though thou shouldst give but a glance at my heart, and see me as one sees a passing meteor moving afar, yet thou wouldst by that glimpse sum up all the meanings of my soul, so transparent is everything to thy piercing glance.[21]

This same emphasis on God's exhaustive and detailed knowledge of the inner man is found in numerous other texts:

"Nothing in all creation is hidden from God's sight. Everything is uncovered and laid bare before the eyes of him to whom we must give account" (Heb. 4:13).

"'And you, my son Solomon, acknowledge the God of your father, and serve him with wholehearted devotion

---

20. Donald Glenn, "An Exegetical and Theological Exposition of Psalm 139," in *Tradition and Testament: Essays in Honor of Charles Lee Feinberg*, edited by John S. Feinberg and Paul D. Feinberg (Chicago: Moody Press, 1981), pp. 171–172.

21. Charles H. Spurgeon, *The Treasury of David* (Grand Rapids: Zondervan, 1976), IIIb:259.

and with a willing mind, for the LORD searches every heart and understands every motive behind the thoughts'" (1 Chron. 28:9a).

"The eyes of the LORD are everywhere, keeping watch on the wicked and the good" (Prov. 15:3).

"The heart is deceitful above all things and beyond cure. Who can understand it? 'I the LORD search the heart and examine the mind, to reward a man according to his conduct, according to what his deeds deserve'" (Jer. 17:9–10; cf. also Jer. 16:17; 1 Kings 8:39).

"You know my folly, O God; my guilt is not hidden from you" (Ps. 69:5).[22]

The third and final aspect wherein God's infinite knowledge is manifest concerns not the inner man but the outer man. That is to say, no journey we take, no path we traverse, no plan we execute, no shelter in which we may hide, is hidden from His sight:

"You hem me in—behind and before; you have laid your hand upon me. Such knowledge is too wonderful for me, too lofty for me to attain" (Ps. 139:5–6).

"Why do you say, O Jacob, and complain, O Israel, 'My way is hidden from the LORD; my cause is disregarded by my God'? Do you not know? Have you not heard? The LORD is the everlasting God, the Creator of the ends of the earth. He will not grow tired or weary, and his understanding no one can fathom" (Isa. 40:27–28).[23]

Foreknowledge and Free Will

The relation between God's omniscience and decree is especially problematic. Yet, the problem is more of human origin than divine, for "this is what God the LORD

22. See also John 21:17; 1 John 3:20; Prov. 15:11; Jer. 11:20; 20:12; Luke 16:15; Acts 1:24; Rom. 8:27; Ps. 94:9–11; Ezek. 11:5; 1 Cor. 3:20; 1 Thess. 2:4; Rev. 2:23; Jer. 18:23; 32:19; 1 Sam. 16:7; Isa. 66:18; Deut. 31:21; John 2:25; Matt. 9:4.

23. See also Job 23:10; 24:23; 31:4; Ps. 1:6; 119:168; 33:13–15; 37:18; Isa. 29:15; 1 Sam. 2:3; Matt. 10:30.

says— . . . 'See, the former things have taken place, and new things I declare; before they spring into being I announce them to you'" (Isa. 42:5, 9; cf. Isa. 44:6–7; 45:21; 46:8–11; Ps. 139:14).

"Both the Old and New Testaments," remarks Carl Henry, "teach that God foreknows the future, that he is prescient of the events and circumstances of the created temporal world. This foreknowledge of the future distinguishes the living God from idols and false gods: 'Who then is like me? . . . let him foretell what will come. . . . Did I not proclaim this and foretell it long ago?' (Isa. 44:7f., NIV)."[24] God knows what will be and thus declares it upon no other ground than that He has foreordained it. The divine foreknowledge is predicated upon the divine foreordination.

To say God can know some future event as contingent (that is, as an event that may or may not occur), is to say He does *not* know if it will *be*, which means that God does not have infallible foreknowledge of all events. God's prior knowledge of human action "Y," for example, is predicated upon His decree of "Y." If "Y" is not—by divine decree— certain to occur, God cannot unfailingly and infallibly know it as an event that will be. Shedd makes this quite clear:

> God cannot foreknow a thing that may or may not be a thing; an event that may or may not be an event. The Arminian, shrinking from this limitation of the divine omniscience, asserts that God can foreknow an *uncertainty;* that is, that he can have foreknowledge, without foreordination. But in this case, there is in reality nothing to be foreknown; there is no *object* of foreknowledge.[25]

If the latter be true, God's foreknowledge is not, in fact, knowledge, but mere conjecture. In order for there to be either knowledge or foreknowledge, Shedd explains,

24. Henry, *God, Revelation and Authority*, V:278.
25. Shedd, *Dogmatic Theology*, I:397–98.

there must be only one actual thing to be known, or foreknown. But in the supposed case of contingency and uncertainty, there are two possible things, either of which may turn out to be an object of knowledge, but neither of which is the one certain and definite object required. There is, therefore, nothing knowable in the case. To know, or foreknow an uncertainty, is to know or foreknow a non-entity.[26]

To this someone may object that since foreknowledge does not itself make the event certain (just as our knowledge does not affect the things we know), it therefore remains contingent, though foreknown. But, as Jonathan Edwards has remarked,

> whether prescience be the thing that *makes* the event necessary or no, it alters not the case. Infallible foreknowledge may prove the necessity of the event foreknown, and yet not be the thing which *causes* the necessity. If the foreknowledge be absolute, this *proves* the event known to be necessary, or proves that 'tis impossible but that the event should be, by some means or other, either by a decree, or some other way, if there be any other way: because . . . 'tis absurd to say, that proposition is known to be certainly and infallibly true, which yet may possibly prove not true.[27]

The objection, then, is based on the false assumption that "nothing can prove, or be an evidence of a thing's being necessary, but that which has a causal influence to make it so."[28]

What is disturbing about all this is that human free will seems to be seriously curtailed, if not altogether obliter-

26. Ibid., I:398.

27. Jonathan Edwards, *Freedom of the Will* edited by Paul Ramsey (New Haven: Yale University Press, 1973), p. 263.

28. Ibid.

ated. Ronald Nash explains why divine omniscience and its concomitant doctrine of foreknowledge yield this problem:

> If the body of true propositions known by an omniscient being includes all true propositions about what human beings will do in the future, a serious consequence for human freedom arises. Obviously, it is impossible for any omniscient being to hold even one false belief. Since God foreknows what Jeff will do at 8 p.m. tomorrow, it appears as though Jeff *must* do what God foreknows he will do. But if Jeff *must* do whatever God knows he will do, in what sense is Jeff's action free? If God foreknows what Jeff will do in the future, does Jeff have the ability not to do what God foreknows? It seems highly unlikely. If Jeff had *that* power (the power to do something other than what God foreknows), then God could have been mistaken. God would have held a false belief in which case God's foreknowledge would have actually been fore-ignorance. But this is clearly impossible. If God has true foreknowledge of what human beings will do in the future, it seems that those actions are determined. But if those actions are not determined and human beings really do have the power either to do something or not, then it seems to follow that God lacks omniscience.[29]

This corollary of divine omniscience evidently is what prompted Donald Bloesch to redefine the concept of divine foreknowledge such that it is scarcely recognizable. Although "God knows the future before it happens," argues Bloesch, "he does not literally know the concrete event until it happens."[30] Bloesh insists that "we cannot affirm a preestablished harmony between the eternal plan of God and the events of history, for this would mean a closed or static universe in which real history and freedom

29. Nash, *The Concept of God,* pp. 51–52.
30. Donald G. Bloesch, *Essentials of Evangelical Theology. Volume One: God, Authority, and Salvation* (San Francisco: Harper & Row, 1978), p. 29.

become illusions."[31] He therefore reduces divine omni-science to a vague "overarching providence."[32]

But, as Carl Henry has observed:

> Old Testament predictions fulfilled in the New are not only general, but also highly specific. Such explicit biblical teaching (e.g., Ps. 139:4,16) contravenes the notion that God does not and cannot foreknow particular future events. If real history and freedom require that God does not know the concrete until it happens, can we any longer declare that eternal bliss awaits every individual who trusts Christ or that condemnation awaits every sinner who rejects him?[33]

Was God caught by surprise when His Son was crucified? Surely not. Indeed, the "concrete" act of putting to death the Messiah was foreknown by God precisely because it was foreordained by Him. Peter tells the crowd: "This man was handed over to you by God's set purpose and fore-knowledge; and you, with the help of wicked men, put him to death by nailing him to the cross" (Acts 2:23).

If that were not clear enough, Peter expands upon this point in the prayer:

> Indeed Herod and Pontius Pilate met together with the Gentiles and the people of Israel in this city to conspire against your holy servant Jesus, whom you anointed. They did what your power and will had decided beforehand should happen (Acts 4:27–28).

I do not intend here to continue with a detailed explanation of the impact of divine omniscience on free will. My opinion is that we have but two options: either God is omniscient and human free will is a myth, or men

31. Ibid., pp. 29–30.
32. Ibid., p. 30.
33. Henry, *God, Revelation and Authority*, V:280.

are wholly free and undetermined and God is ignorant. I prefer the former (as I believe it is taught in Scripture) and have defended it at length elsewhere.[34]

"Impossible," Undecreed Events

We often hear that not only does God know all things that *do* occur (obviously, since He has decreed them), He also knows all things that *might have* occurred, had certain conditions been met or circumstances realized (the knowledge of intelligence as earlier defined).

For example, consider the following: "Then Jesus began to denounce the cities in which most of his miracles had been performed, because they did not repent. 'Woe to you, Korazin! Woe to you, Bethsaida! If the miracles that were performed in you had been performed in Tyre and Sidon, they would have repented long ago in sackcloth and ashes. But I tell you, it will be more bearable for Tyre and Sidon on the day of judgment than for you" (Matt. 11:20–22; cf. Matt. 11:23–24; Sam. 23:10–14; Gen. 11:6).

Is this, then, a valid conception of God's knowledge? In a certain sense, yes; but we must be careful. As already explained, God has infallible and certain knowledge of all events because He has decreed that they shall infallibly and certainly occur. But to say that God has knowledge of what *would* have occurred *if* certain conditions had been met or circumstances realized is misleading, for in point of fact God has *not* decreed that such conditions or circumstances should transpire. Hence the events contingent thereupon *cannot* occur, and thus are not objects of God's foreknowledge, being nonentities. Such impossible events can be said to be known by God or to be objects of His knowledge only in *that* sense—as *impossible events* which could have occurred *only* had God so decreed that they

---

34. C. Samuel Storms, "Jonathan Edwards on the Freedom of the Will," *TrinJ* 3 NS (1982):131–169.

occur, which He did not. Or, yet again, God knows them, but He knows them for precisely what they are: impossible events, because undecreed events.

Provocation to Worship, Humility, Holiness, Comfort

The doctrine of divine omniscience is immeasurably relevant to the day-to-day experience of the believer. If ever there existed an opportunity to shatter the silly notion that theology is barren and devoid of practical benefits, this is it.

Can God be worshiped and adored as He ought in ignorance of this attribute? Surely not. Writes Stephen Charnock:

> Consider how great it is to know the thoughts, and intentions, and works of one man from the beginning to the end of his life; to foreknow all these before the being of this man, when he was lodged afar off in the loins of his ancestors, yea, of Adam. How much greater is it to foreknow and know the thoughts and works of three or four men, of a whole village or neighbourhood! It is greater still to know the imaginations and actions of such a multitude of men as are contained in London, Paris, or Constantinople; how much greater still to know the intentions and practices, the clandestine contrivances of so many millions, that have, do, or shall swarm in all quarters of the world, every person of them having millions of thoughts, desires, designs, affections, and actions! Let this attribute, then, make the blessed God honourable in our eyes and adorable in all our affections. . . . *Adore God for this wonderful perfection*(!).[35]

The divine omniscience is also a provocation to humility. In the light of this incomparable excellency in God,

35. Stephen Charnock, *The Existence and Attributes of God* (Grand Rapids: Sovereign Grace, 1971), pp. 239–40. *Emphasis mine.*

what low thoughts ought we to have of ourselves. As Charnock elaborates:

> There is nothing man is more apt to be proud of than his knowledge; it is a perfection he glories in; but if our own knowledge of the little outside and barks of things puffs us up, the consideration of the infiniteness of God's knowledge should abate the tumour. As our beings are nothing in regard to the infiniteness of his essence, so our knowledge is nothing in regard of the vastness of his understanding. We have a spark of being, but nothing to the heat of the sun; we have a drop of knowledge, but nothing to the divine ocean. What a vain thing is it for a shallow brook to boast of its streams, before a sea whose depths are unfathomable! As it is a vanity to brag of our strength when we remember the power of God, and of our prudence when we glance upon the wisdom of God, so it is no less a vanity to boast of our knowledge when we think of the understanding and knowledge of God.[36]

I have already spoken of the knowledge God has of the inner man, of what we believe are the "secrets" of the heart. Could there be a more effective incentive to holiness? Charnock asks:

> Can a man's conscience easily and delightfully swallow that which he is sensible falls under the cognizance of God, when it is hateful to the eye of his holiness, and renders the actor odious to him? . . . Temptations have no encouragement to come near him that is constantly armed with the thoughts that his sin is booked in God's omniscience.[37]

What is more glorious yet is that this doctrine which makes us fearful of sin is also the foundation of comfort and assurance. If God is omniscient (and He surely is), then

36. Ibid., p. 240.
37. Ibid., p. 258.

He knows the worst about us, but loves us notwithstanding! The apostle John writes: "This then is how we know that we belong to the truth, and how we set our hearts at rest in his presence whenever our hearts condemn us. For God is greater than our hearts, and he knows everything" (1 John 3:19–20).

And what possible reason do we have for being impatient, inasmuch as God knows our needs and wants before we do? (Matt. 6:8, 32).

Finally, our trust and our hope shall not disappoint, for they are in Him who knows all things. Charnock observes:

> This perfection of God fits him to be a special object of trust. If he were forgetful, what comfort could we have in any promise? How could we depend upon him if he were ignorant of our state? His compassions to pity us, his readiness to relieve us, his power to protect and assist us, would be insignificant, without his omniscience to inform his goodness and direct the arm of his power. . . . You may depend upon his mercy that hath promised, and upon his truth to perform, upon his sufficiency to supply you and his goodness to relieve you, and his righteousness to reward you, because he hath an infinite understanding to know you and your wants, you and your services.[38]

38. Ibid., p. 249.

5

Here, There, and Everywhere

Omnipresence

The "omni's" of God, if I may refer to them in this way, are of little comfort to the rebellious heart, for they shatter those illusions on the strength of which we so often justify our sin. Thinking that none has access to the secrets of our hearts, we lust, envy, hate, and covet. But what we naively think to have concealed successfully behind the veil of the soul is but an open book before Him with whom we have to do:

> O LORD, you have searched me and you know me. You know when I sit and when I rise; you perceive my thoughts from afar. You discern my going out and my lying down; you are familiar with all my ways. Before a word is on my tongue you know it completely, O LORD (Ps. 139:1–4).

But might there not be some secluded hideaway, some remote corner of the universe to which even the Deity has no access? Might we not *there* sin freely? Might we not *there* sin secretly? But *where* is "there"?

> Where can I go from your Spirit? Where can I flee from your presence? If I go up to the heavens, you are there; if I make my bed in the depths, you are there. If I rise on the wings of

the dawn, if I settle on the far side of the sea, even there
your hand will guide me, your right hand will hold me fast.
If I say, "Surely the darkness will hide me and the light
become night around me," even the darkness will not be
dark to you; the night will shine like the day, for darkness is
as light to you (Ps. 139:7–12).

It is not merely the omniscience of God but His omnipresence as well, noted Charles Spurgeon, that makes it
dreadful work to sin,

for we offend the Almighty to his face, and commit acts of
treason at the very foot of his throne. *Go* from him, or *flee*
from him we cannot: neither by patient travel nor by hasty
flight can we withdraw from the all-surrounding Deity. His
mind is in our mind; himself within ourselves. His spirit is
over our spirit; our presence is ever in his presence.[1]

Inexhaustibly Infinite in Space

When we speak of God as infinite, we mean that He is
without limit, that He is in all relevant respects inexhaustible, subject to no conceivable calculations, in no way
saddled by the imperfections of the creature. Infinity, in
sum, is that in virtue of which the Deity embraces all His
perfections in the highest degree. Infinity may thus be
predicated of God in several ways. God is infinite, for
example, in relation to time, knowledge, power and space.
To say that God is infinite with respect to time is to
predicate "eternity" of the Divine Being (He is everlasting,
without beginning or end). To say that God is infinite with
respect to knowledge, as we have just seen, is to predicate
"omniscience" of the Divine Being (He knows all things,
and that infallibly). To say that God is infinite with respect
to power (as we shall see in the next chapter) is to

1. Charles H. Spurgeon, *The Treasury of David* (Grand Rapids: Zondervan,
1976), IIIb:260.

predicate "omnipotence" of the Divine Being. But in this chapter we shall speak of God as infinite with respect to space and thus predicate of Him "omnipresence" and "immensity."

A slight distinction between "immensity" and "omnipresence" ought to be noted. Whereas immensity affirms that God transcends all spatial limitations, that His being cannot be contained or localized, omnipresence signifies more specifically the relationship which God in His whole being sustains to the creation itself. In other words, *omnipresence* (being positive in thrust) means that God is everywhere present in the world; *immensity* (being negative in thrust) means that He is by no means limited to or confined by it.

God, of course, is not "in space" in the sense that, say, we or the angelic host are. We who have material bodies are bounded by space and thus can always be said to be here and not there, or there and not here. That is, a body occupies *a* place *in* space. Angelic spirits, on the other hand, as well as the dead in Christ now in the intermediate state, are not bound by space and yet they are somewhere, not everywhere. But God, and God alone, fills all space. He is not absent from any portion of space, nor more present in one portion than in another.

Essentially and Wholly Present

The teaching of Scripture on God's omnipresence is unassailable. In addition to what we have already seen in Psalm 139, note the following:

" 'Can anyone hide in secret places so that I cannot see him?' declares the LORD. 'Do not I fill heaven and earth?' declares the LORD" (Jer. 23:24).

"But will God really dwell on earth? The heavens, even the highest heaven, cannot contain you. How much less this temple I have built!" (1 Kings 8:27; see also 2 Chron. 2:6; Isa. 66:1).

"And God placed all things under his feet and appointed him to be head over everything for the church, which is his body, the fullness of him who fills everything in every way" (Eph. 1:22–23).

"For in him we live and move and have our being" (Acts 17:28a).

"He is before all things, and in him all things hold together" (Col. 1:17).

Several aspects of God's omnipresence call for comment. In the first place, God is omnipresent according to His being and not merely according to His operation. That is to say, He is *essentially* or *substantially*, not only dynamically, omnipresent. It is the heresy of deism which contends that God is present in all places only by way of influence and power, acting upon the world from a distance, but not *Himself* wholly present throughout. As Bavinck explains,

> God is not present in creation as a king in his realm or a captain aboard his ship. He does not act upon the world from a distance; but with his whole being he is present powerfully here and everywhere with respect to his essence and power.[2]

Second, although God is wholly present throughout all things, He is yet distinct from all things. It does not follow that because God is essentially *in* everything that everything *is* essentially God. It is the heresy of pantheism that the being of God is one and the same with the being of all reality. Pantheism asserts that God minus the world = 0; theism asserts that God minus the world = God. The universe is the creation of God and thus, in respect to essence, no part of Him. The creation is ontologically other than God, a product *ex nihilo* of the divine will, not an extension of the Divine Being itself. Consequently, al-

---

2. Herman Bavinck, *The Doctrine of God*, translated, edited and outlined by William Hendriksen (Edinburgh: The Banner of Truth Trust, 1977), p. 162.

though all things are permeated and sustained in being by God (Col. 1: 16–17; Acts 17:28), God is not all things.

Third, this presence of God throughout the whole of space is not by local diffusion, multiplication, or distribution. Being wholly spirit, God is not subject to the laws of matter such as extension and displacement. He cannot be divided or separated such that one part of His being is here and not there, and another part there and not here. The whole of His being is always everywhere, no less nor more here than there, or there than here. J. L. Dagg comments:

> God is indivisible. We cannot say, that a part of his essence is here, and a part yonder. If this were the mode of God's omnipresence in universal space, he would be infinitely divided, and only an infinitely small part of him would be present at each place. It would not be the whole deity, that takes cognizance of our actions, and listens to our petitions. This notion is unfavorable to piety, and opposed to the true sense of Scripture: "The eyes of the Lord are in every place, beholding the evil and the good."[3]

Finally, whereas the presence of a body in *a* place of space excludes the simultaneous and in all ways identical presence of another body in the same place of space, such is not true of the Divine Being. God *is*, in the whole of His being, *where* everything else *is* (including matter). Substance or matter is in no way displaced or spatially excluded by the presence of God. To put it bluntly, when God created all things out of nothing, He did not have to "move out of the way" to make room for the world. He is where it is.

The Limitations of Human Metaphors

The doctrine of God's omnipresence is not without its problems. For example, if God is everywhere present, and

---

3. J. L. Dagg, *A Manual of Theology* (Harrisonburg: Gano Books, 1982), p. 61.

that equally, in what sense can He be said to "indwell" or "abide in" the Christian but not the non-Christian? Paul affirms that you "are controlled not by the sinful nature but by the Spirit, if the Spirit of God lives in you" (Rom. 8:9a). And again, "if the Spirit of him who raised Jesus from the dead is living in you, he who raised Christ from the dead will also give life to your mortal bodies through his Spirit, who lives in you" (Rom. 8:11). It was Jesus who said, "If anyone loves me, he will obey my teaching. My Father will love him, and we will come to him and make our home with him" (John 14:23). It is in Christ, Paul reminds us, that we are "being built together to become a dwelling in which God lives by his Spirit" (Eph. 2:22). Christ Himself "dwells" in our hearts through faith (Eph. 3:17). And what is the mystery now disclosed to the saints? It is "Christ in you, the hope of glory" (Col. 1:27).

Similarly, if God is wholly everywhere present, what can it mean to say the Spirit "descended" at Pentecost or "fell upon" believers (cf. Acts 1:8; 2:17; 10:44–48)? The same question is asked concerning those texts which speak of heaven as the abode of God. For example:

Look down from heaven, your holy dwelling place, and bless your people Israel and the land you have given us as you promised on oath to our forefathers, a land flowing with milk and honey" (Deut. 26:15).
From heaven the LORD looks down and sees all mankind; from his dwelling place he watches all who live on earth" (Ps. 33:13–14; see also Ps. 11:4; 115:3).

The portrayal of God in heaven is not as difficult as it may appear. Clearly, the point of such descriptive statements is not to deny God's presence upon the earth, or anywhere else for that matter. Rather, it is to emphasize the ethical and ontological transcendence of God vis-á-vis the creature. It is His holiness, His wholly-otherness if you will, that is being magnified. According to A. H. Strong, "When

God is said to 'dwell in the heavens,' we are to understand the language either as a symbolic expression of exaltation above earthly things, or as a declaration that his most special and glorious self-manifestations are to the spirits of heaven."[4]

The other statements noted above, however, are not so readily intelligible. The Baptist theologian J. L. Dagg attempted to explain the problem in this way:

> There are passages of Scripture which speak of God's removing from one place to another; of his approaching and departing; of his dwelling in heaven, and of his coming near to his people, and taking up his abode with them. These are manifestly accommodations of language; just as when eyes or hands are attributed to him. They refer to the manifestations of his presence in his various works, and dispensations, in which such changes take place, as are appropriately and impressively expressed by this language.[5]

Likewise, J. O. Buswell insisted that we interpret statements concerning God's coming and going as "anthropomorphic expressions" which are "clearly figurative."[6]

Berkhof contends that although God is present in every part of His creation, He is *not* equally present in the same sense in all His creatures:

> . . . the nature of His indwelling is in harmony with that of His creatures. He does not dwell on earth as He does in heaven, in animals as He does in man, in the inorganic as He does in the organic creation, in the wicked as He does in the pious, nor in the Church as He does in Christ. There is an endless variety in the manner in which He is immanent

4. A. H. Strong, *Systematic Theology* (Old Tappan: Fleming H. Revell, 1970), p. 280.

5. Dagg, *A Manual of Theology*, p. 61.

6. James O. Buswell, *A Systematic Theology of the Christian Religion* (Grand Rapids: Zondervan, 1973), I:37.

in His creatures, and in the measure in which they reveal God to those who have eyes to see.[7]

Unfortunately, Berkhof does not tell us in what sense God's presence differs. A. A. Hodge attempts to do this by conceiving of God's presence according to several different modes. In respect to essence and knowledge, He is present the same everywhere and always. However,

> as to his self-manifestation and the exercise of his power, his presence differs endlessly in different cases in degree and mode. Thus God is present to the church as he is not to the world. Thus he is present in hell in the manifestation and execution of righteous wrath, while he is present in heaven in the manifestation and communication of gracious love and glory.[8]

Similarly, according to Shedd, "God is said to be 'in heaven,' 'in believers,' 'in hell,' etc. because of a special manifestation of his glory, or his grace, or his retribution."[9]

Does this mean, for example, that whereas the gracious God is *in* the unbeliever, He is not in him "graciously"? That is to say, God's perfect presence in all need not entail the same manifestation of divine power. His indwelling of the Christian is in some sense qualitatively different from His presence in the non-Christian. It is not simply a "spatial" but also a "spiritual" presence, such that distinctive divine blessings and operations are dispensed only in the believer. "Indwelling," therefore, is something of a metaphor designed to emphasize the unique personal and salvific relationship the Christian sustains to God, be it the new life bestowed and nourished, the new power by which

7. Louis Berkhof, *Systematic Theology* (Grand Rapids: Wm. B. Eerdmans, 1972), p. 61.

8. A. A. Hodge, *Outlines of Theology* (London: The Banner of Truth Trust, 1972), p. 141.

9. William G. T. Shedd, *Dogmatic Theology* (Minneapolis: Klock & Klock Christian Publishers, 1979), I:341.

obedience is now possible, or whatever. Thus to be "far" from God is not to be spatially at a distance but ethically and relationally incongruous with Him. Thus, drawing "near" to God does not require a journey, only repentance, faith, and humility (cf. Isa. 57:15; 59:2; Prov. 15:29).

This attempt at resolving the problem of God's omnipresence and His "special" presence is not entirely satisfactory. Few, if any, of the terms I have used are precisely accurate in drawing what we know are legitimate biblical distinctions. However, we *know* that the Holy Spirit "indwells" Christians but not the lost. We *know* that God does give Christians a divine and supernatural enablement by virtue of His indwelling Spirit which He does not make available to the unbeliever. We *know* that at the second advent the unrepentant will be punished "with everlasting destruction and shut out from the presence of the Lord and from the majesty of his power" (2 Thess. 1:9), whereas we who believe shall abide with Him forever. These verities are clear enough. We *know* what they entail. Our inability to reconcile them in every respect with God's omnipresence is due only to our limitations, and in no way detracts from their eternal validity.

Both Warning and Consolation

The doctrine of God's omnipresence, as I mentioned at the beginning of this chapter, is of immeasurable practical benefit. It is, first of all, a stern warning to the wicked, as Charnock elaborates:

How terrible should the thoughts of this attribute be to sinners! How foolish is it to imagine any hiding-place from the incomprehensible God, who fills and contains all things, and is present in every point of the world. When men have shut the door, and made all darkness within, to meditate or commit a crime, they cannot in the most intricate recesses be sheltered from the presence of God. If they could separate themselves from their own shadows, they could not avoid his company, or be obscured from his sight: Ps. cxxxix. 12, "The darkness and light are both alike to him." Hypocrites cannot disguise their sentiments from him; he is in the most secret nook of their hearts. No thought is hid, no lust is secret, but the eye of God beholds this, and that, and the other. He is present with our heart when we imagine, with our hands when we act. We may exclude the sun from peeping into our solitudes, but not the eyes of God from beholding our actions.[10]

If God's omnipresence frightens the wicked, it should console the righteous. No matter what the trial, no matter the place of its occurrence, no matter the swiftness with which it assaults, no matter the depth of its power, *God is ever with us!* His loving protection ever abides. "Even though I walk through the valley of the shadow of death, I will fear no evil, *for you are with me;* your rod and your staff, they comfort me" (Ps. 23:4).

Finally, Charnock reminds us of what a glorious and powerful incentive to holiness is the truth of God's omnipresence:

What man would do an unworthy action, or speak an unhandsome word in the presence of his prince? The eye of the general inflames the spirit of a soldier. Why did David "keep God's testimonies"? Because he considered that "all his ways were before him," Ps. cxix. 168; because he was persuaded his ways were present with God, God's precepts should be present with him. The same was the cause of Job's integrity; "doth he not see my ways?" Job xxxi. 4; to have God in our eye is the way to be sincere, "walk before me," as in my sight, "and be thou perfect," Gen. xvii. 1. Communion with God consists chiefly in an ordering our ways as in the presence of him that is

10. Stephen Charnock, *The Existence and Attributes of God* (Grand Rapids: Sovereign Grace, 1971), p. 174.

invisible. This would make us spiritual, raised and watchful in all our passions, if we considered that God is present with us in our shops, in our chambers, in our walks, and in our meetings, as present with us as with the angels in heaven; who though they have a presence of glory above us, yet have not a greater measure of his essential presence than we have.[11]

11. Ibid., p. 179.

6

God and Round Triangles

Omnipotence

A highly simplistic definition of "power" would be that it is the ability to produce effects, or to accomplish what one wills. The Scriptures heartily affirm not only that God has such an ability, but that He has it without limitations. Hence, we speak of God as being *omnipotent*, infinite in power.

His "power is vast" (Job 9:4). He is "the Lord strong and mighty" (Ps. 24:8), "great and awesome" (Deut. 7:21), "the Lord Almighty, the Mighty One of Israel" (Isa. 1:24). "Ah, Sovereign Lord, you have made the heavens and the earth by your great power and outstretched arm. Nothing is too hard for you. You show love to thousands but bring the punishment for the father's sins into the laps of their children after them. O great and powerful God, whose name is the Lord Almighty, great are your purposes and mighty are your deeds" (Jer. 32:17–19a). Creation is a testimony to "his great power and mighty strength" (Isa. 40:26). He is Lord, Owner, Ruler, and King of all creation, whom none can resist or overpower (Matt. 11:25; Rev. 1:8; Ps. 29:10; Jer. 10:7, 10). He is "the Lord Almighty" (2 Cor. 6:18; Rev. 4:8; 11:17), "the blessed and only Ruler, the King of kings and Lord of lords" (1 Tim. 6:15). Nothing is too difficult for Him; all things are within His power (Gen. 18:14; Zech. 8:6; Jer. 32:27; Matt. 19:26; Luke 1:37). Whatever He pleases, that He does (Ps. 115:3; 135:6; Isa. 14:24, 27; 46:10; 55:11). "Then Job replied to the Lᴏʀᴅ: 'I know that you can do all things; no plan of yours can be thwarted'" (Job 42:1–2).

Power Without Limit

The divine power is optional in its exercise. Whereas God *is* power in His eternal being, it is not a necessary constituent of God's being that He always and in every way exercise His power. In other words, as Shedd explains, "God need not have created anything. And after creation, he may annihilate. Only when he has bound himself by promise, as in the instance of faith in Christ, does his action cease to be optional."[1]

Furthermore, God accomplishes His will in one of two ways—either (1) by appointed means, i.e., by the uniform and ordered operation of second causes, or (2) without appointed means or second causes, i.e., by divine fiat. Included under (1) would be all activities of God's providential government whereby use is made of existing things. God in providence employs the creation itself and the "laws of nature" (which are but the will of God applied to creation) to carry out His purpose (e.g., sustaining human life by means of food and water; providing warmth for our atmosphere via the heat of the sun). According to Shedd, "The First cause [God] uses second causes [the creation] previously originated ex nihilo."[2] Included under (2) would be all things which God effects by an immediate act of His will. No use is made of anything already in

---

1. William G. T. Shedd, *Dogmatic Theology* (Minneapolis: Klock & Klock Christian Publishers, 1979), I:359.
   2. Ibid., I:362.

existence. Creation, for example, as well as miracles are of this order of divine power: they are actions which are the operation of the first cause alone.

We should also remember that the actual exercise of God's power does not represent its limits. God *can* do all He wills (and does), but *need not* do (and does not) all He can. That is to say, God's infinite power is *manifested* in the works of creation, but is *not exhausted* by them. God could have created more than He has, if He so pleased. What God *has* done, therefore, is no measure of what He *could* have done or can do. This is important in that it guards against the suggestion that if God did *not* do it, it is because He *cannot* do it. As Charnock notes:

> that the objects of divine power are innumerable, appears, because God can do infinitely more than he hath done or will do. Nothing that God hath done can enfeeble or dull his power; there still resides in him an ability beyond all the settled contrivances of his understanding and resolves of his will, which no effects which he hath wrought can drain and put to a stand.[3]

Power Without Self-Contradiction

Can God do anything and everything? This question has been answered both affirmatively and negatively.

Certain medieval scholastic theologians and later philosophers such as René Descartes argued that God has an absolute power in the sense of a power free from, indeed often contradictory to, all reason and morality. Thus, they concluded that God can sin,[4] lie, and die, among other

---

3. Stephen Charnock, *The Existence and Attributes of God* (Grand Rapids: Sovereign Grace, 1971), p. 370.

4. Surprisingly, Stephen Davis in *Logic and the Nature of God* (Grand Rapids: Wm. B. Eerdmans, 1983) insists that God *can* sin: otherwise, Davis argues, we would have no good reason to praise Him for His moral goodness! See pp. 93–96.

things. He is not only able to do all He wills, but He is able also to will everything, even the logically contradictory.

Most theologians, on the other hand, have pointed to several texts of Scripture which call for a negative response to the question. For example:

"Because God wanted to make the unchanging nature of his purpose very clear to the heirs of what was promised, he confirmed it with an oath. God did this so that, by two unchangeable things in which it is impossible for God to lie, we who have fled to take hold of the hope offered to us may be greatly encouraged" (Heb. 6:17–18).

"If we are faithless, he will remain faithful, for he cannot disown himself" (2 Tim. 2:13).

"When tempted, no one should say, 'God is tempting me.' For God cannot be tempted by evil, nor does he tempt anyone" (James 1:13).

Charles Hodge explains:

> It is . . . involved in the very idea of power, that it has reference to the production of possible effects. It is no more a limitation of power that it cannot effect the impossible, than it is of reason that it cannot comprehend the absurd, or of infinite goodness that it cannot do wrong. It is contrary to its nature. Instead of exalting, it degrades God, to suppose that He can be other than He is, or that He can act contrary to infinite wisdom and love. When, therefore, it is said that God is omnipotent because He can do whatever He wills, it is to be remembered that His will is determined by His nature. It is certainly no limitation to perfection to say that it cannot be imperfect.[5]

Augustine concurs: "God is omnipotent, and yet he cannot die, he cannot lie, he cannot deny himself. How is he omnipotent then? He is omnipotent for the very reason

5. Charles Hodge, *Systematic Theology* (Grand Rapids: Wm. B. Eerdmans, 1970), I:409.

that he cannot do these things. For if he could die, he would not be omnipotent."[6]

How is it that to say God *cannot* do something is power, and to say God *can* do something else, is weakness? Augustine answers: "The power of God is not diminished when it is said that he cannot die, and cannot sin; for if he could do these things, his power would be less. A being is rightly called omnipotent, from doing what he wills, and not from suffering what he does not will."[7]

What Augustine is saying is this: to be able to do all that one wills to do is to be omnipotent. But to be unable to do what one does *not* will to do is not weakness, for power is the ability to do one's will, not the ability to do what is not one's will. Ronald Nash puts it yet another way: "The power to sin is the power to fall short of perfection. Since this is the opposite of omnipotence, God's inability to sin is not inconsistent with His omnipotence; rather, it is entailed by His omnipotence."[8]

Whereas both Hodge and Augustine are correct, in yet another sense it must be said that God *can*, in fact, do everything. This calls for some explanation. When I say God can do everything, someone will respond by pointing out that God cannot do the logically absurd or self-contradictory. For example, this objector would say: "God cannot create a round triangle!" But a round triangle is a nonentity, a nothing. To say that "something" is round at the same time and in the same sense in which it is triangular is to utter a contradiction. Such contradictions do not exist, indeed cannot exist, in fact cannot even be conceived of as existing. It is, of course, possible to conceive of the sentence "Here is a round triangle." But it

6. This is a paraphrase of Augustine's comments in his *On the Creed; The Nicene and Post-Nicene Fathers*, edited by Philip Schaff (Grand Rapids: Wm. B. Eerdmans, 1956), III:369.

7. This, too, is a paraphrase of Augustine's response in *The City of God,* V:10; ibid., II:92.

8. Ronald Nash, *The Concept of God* (Grand Rapids: Zondervan, 1983), p. 40.

is not possible to conceive of a "round triangle" as actually existing. If you think you can conceive of one, describe it to me. What does a round triangle look like? Therefore, God's supposed "inability" to create a round triangle is not a result of His being limited by uncreated conditions in the universe. Rather, it is an inability to do nothing, since that is precisely what a round triangle is: nothing. And to say that God is unable to do "nothing" is a meaningless assertion. Consequently, God can do everything. Richard Swinburne concludes:

> A logically impossible action is not an action. It is what is described by a form of words which purport to describe an action, but do not describe anything which it is coherent to suppose could be done. It is no objection to A's omnipotence that he cannot make a square circle [or a round triangle]. This is because "making a square circle" does not describe anything which it is coherent to suppose could be done.[9]

In the light of this, Carl Henry concludes, and I concur:

> That God will not alter his own nature, that he cannot deny himself, that he cannot lie and cannot sin, that he cannot be deceived, and that, moreover, he cannot die, are affirmations which historic Christian theology has always properly associated with divine omnipotence and not with divine limitation or divine impotency, because the "possibility" as stated is a logical impossibility. Any conception of omnipotence that requires God to contradict himself reflects a conjectural and ridiculous notion of absolute power.[10]

The objection that this puts God in subservience to the laws of logic, as if to say He is restricted by something external to Himself, fails to realize that "the laws of logic

9. Richard Swinburne, *The Coherence of Theism* (Oxford: Clarendon Press, 1977), p. 149.
10. Carl F. H. Henry, *God, Revelation and Authority* (Waco: Word Books, 1982), V:319.

are the way God thinks; they are the organization of the
divine mind."[11] Moreover, and more immediately relevant
to the concerns of the Christian is the fact that—according
to Ronald Nash—

> if God can do self-contradictory acts, then there is no
> inconsistency in His *promising* eternal life to all who trust
> in Christ but actually condemning to everlasting damna-
> tion all who trust in Christ. Such duplicity (inconsistency)
> would be entirely in character for a God not bound by the
> law of noncontradiction since, in a world where the law
> does not apply, there is no difference between eternal life
> and eternal damnation.[12]

The same approach may be taken in dealing with the
age-old conundrum whether God can create a stone too
heavy for God to lift. Nash articulates the problem:

> If God can create the stone too heavy for God to lift, there is
> something God cannot do (namely, lift the stone). And if
> God cannot create the stone too heavy for Him to lift, there
> is still something He cannot do (in this case, create the
> stone). Either God can or cannot create such a stone.
> Therefore, in either case, there is something God cannot
> do; and in either case, we seem forced to conclude that God
> is not omnipotent.[13]

But again, for this objection to hold, it must propose a
"thing," a genuine "task" for God to do. But it does not. The
request that "the Being who can do anything, which
includes creating and lifting all stones, create a stone too
heavy to be lifted by the Being who can lift any created
thing" is incoherent. It proposes nothing. It is a pseudo-
task. That is to say, a stone too heavy to be lifted by Him
who can lift all stones is contradictory. Likewise, for God

11. Ibid.
12. Nash, *The Concept of God*, pp. 40–41.
13. Ibid., p. 47.

to create something which is a nothing (namely, a stone
too heavy to be lifted by Him who can lift all stones), is
contradictory. That God cannot create a stone which
logically cannot be created is no more a threat to omnipotence than his alleged "inability" to create a round triangle. Thus, praise be to God who can do all things!

An Assurance of Salvation

God's omnipotence is manifested in any number of
ways. It is seen in creation (Ps. 33:6; Ps. 19; Gen. 1:1ff.; Isa.
45:12; Rom. 1:20; etc.); in preservation (Col. 1:17); in providence (Heb. 1:3); in redemption (Rom. 1:16; 2 Cor. 1:22–24;
Eph. 3:20–21); and in judgment (Rom. 9:22).

His omnipotence, as we have seen with omniscience
and omnipresence, is also of immense practical significance. It is, in the first place, a reason for praise and
worship. In Charnock's view:

> Wisdom and power are the grounds of the respect we give
> to men; they being both infinite in God, are the foundation
> of a solemn honour to be returned to him by his creatures.
> If a man make a curious engine, we honour him for his
> skill; if another vanquish a vigorous enemy, we admire him
> for his strength; and shall not the efficacy of God's power in
> creation, government, redemption, inflame us with a sense
> of the honour of his name and perfections! We admire
> those princes that have vast empires, numerous armies,
> that have a power to conquer their enemies, and preserve
> their own people in peace; how much more ground have
> we to pay a mighty reverence to God, who, without trouble
> and weariness, made and manages this vast empire of the
> world by a word and beck! What sensible thoughts have we
> of the noise of thunder, the power of the sun, the storms of
> the sea! These things, that have no understanding, have
> struck men with such a reverence that many have adored
> them as gods. What reverence and adoration doth this

mighty power, joined with an infinite wisdom in God, demand at our hands![14]

This attribute is an especially ominous warning to those who think they somehow can resist God's judgment. "How foolish is every sinner! Can we poor worms strut it out against infinite power?"[15] Oh, that every obstinate sinner, pleads Charnock,

> would think of this, and consider his unmeasurable bold-ness in thinking himself able to grapple with omnipotence! What force can any have to resist the presence of him before whom rocks melt, and the heavens at length shall be shrivelled up as a parchment by the last fire! As the light of God's face is too dazzling to be beheld by us, so the arm of his power is too mighty to be opposed by us.[16]

But like all the other excellencies of God, omnipotence is even more a comfort to those who are His children. It is a comfort to them when persecuted and oppressed: "The LORD is my light and my salvation—whom shall I fear? The LORD is the stronghold of my life—of whom shall I be afraid?" (Ps. 27:1).

It is a comfort and encouragement when we are beset by temptations: "No temptation has seized you except what is common to man. And God is faithful; he will not let you be tempted beyond what you can bear. But when you are tempted, he will also provide a way out so that you can stand up against it" (1 Cor. 10:13).

God's infinite ability to answer prayer is affirmed by Paul (Eph. 3:20–21) in a most glorious way. John Stott explains:

> (1) He is able to *do* or to work *(poiēsai)*, for he is neither idle, nor inactive, nor dead. (2) He is able to do what *we ask*, for

14. Charnock, *The Existence and Attributes of God*, p. 429.
15. Ibid., p. 436.
16. Ibid., p. 437.

he hears and answers prayer. (3) He is able to do what we ask *or think*, for he reads our thoughts, and sometimes we imagine things for which we dare not and therefore do not ask. (4) He is able to do *all* that we ask or think, for he knows it all and can perform it all. (5) He is able to do *more . . . than (hyper,* "beyond") all that we ask or think, for his expectations are higher than ours. (6) He is able to do much more, or *more abundantly (perissōs),* than all that we ask or think, for he does not give his grace by calculated measure. (7) He is able to do very much more, *far more abundantly,* than all that we ask or think, for he is a God of super-abundance.[17]

There is yet more! We may be strengthened in knowing that *all* He has promised He *will,* because He *can,* fulfill (Jude 24–25). It is God's infinite and incomparable power, among other things, on which our assurance of salvation is based:

> I give them eternal life, and they shall never perish, no one can snatch them out of my hand. My Father, who has given them to me, is greater than all; no one can snatch them out of my Father's hand (John 10:28-29; see also Rom. 8:31–39).

With the twenty-four elders we can but exclaim:

> You are worthy, our Lord and God, to receive glory and honor and power, for you have created all things, and by your will they were created and have their being (Rev. 4:11).

17. John R. W. Stott, *God's New Society: The Message of Ephesians* (Downers Grove: InterVarsity Press, 1979), pp. 139–40.

Great Is Thy Faithfulness

Immutability

The importance of defining our theological terms with precision is most evident in the case of divine immutability. Here is a word which in contemporary evangelical circles evokes either protest or praise. Some see it as a threat to the biblical portrait of God who *does* indeed change: He changes His mind ("repents") and He changes His mode of being ("the Word became flesh"). Others are equally concerned that a careless tampering with this attribute of God will reduce Him to a fickle, unfaithful, and ultimately unworthy object of our affection and worship. It is imperative, therefore, that in the subsequent study we proceed cautiously, and yet with conviction, in the explanation of the sense in which God both can and cannot change.

Consistency in Scripture

The immutability of God is related to, but clearly distinct from, His eternity. In saying that God is eternal, in the sense of everlasting, we mean that He always has and always will exist. He was preceded by nothing and shall be succeeded by nothing. In saying that God is immutable we mean that He is consistently the same in His eternal being. The Being, who eternally is, never changes.

This affirmation of unchangeableness, however, is not designed to deny that there is change and development in God's *relations* to His creatures. We who were once His enemies are now by the grace of Christ His friends (Rom. 5:6–11). The God who declared His intention to destroy Nineveh for its sin "changed" His mind upon its repentance (more on this later). Furthermore, this affirmation of immutability must not be interpreted in such a way that the reality of the "Word become flesh" is threatened (John 1:14). We must acknowledge (our salvation depends upon it) that He who *is* in His eternal being *very God* became, in space-time history, *very man*. Yet the Word who *became* flesh did not cease to be the Word (no transubstantiation here!). The second person of the Trinity has taken unto Himself or assumed a human nature, yet without alteration or reduction of His essential deity. He is now what He has always been: very God. He is now what He once was not: very man. He is now—and forever will be—both: the God-man. It is a simplistic and ill-conceived doctrine of immutability that denies any part of this essential biblical verity. Thus, to say *without qualification* that God cannot change or that He can and often does change is at best unwise, at worst misleading. Our concept of immutability must be formulated in such a way that we do justice to every biblical assertion concerning both the "being" and "becoming" of God.

Clearly, then, to say that God is immutable is not to say that He is immobile or static, for whereas all change is activity, not all activity is change. It is simply to affirm that God always is and acts in perfect harmony with the revelation of Himself and His will in Scripture. For example, Scripture tells us that God is good, just, and loving. Immutability, or constancy, simply asserts that when the exigencies of a situation call for goodness, justice, or love as the appropriate response on the part of the Deity, that is precisely what God will be (or do, as the case may be). To say the same thing, but negatively, if God ought to be good, just, or loving as the circumstances may demand, He will by no means ever be evil, unfair, or hateful. Immutability means that the God who in Scripture is said to be omnipresent, omniscient, and omnipotent, has not, is not, and never will be—under any and all imaginable circumstances—localized, ignorant, or impotent.[1] *What* He is, He *always* is.

To be more specific, God is immutable in respect to His (1) essential being (God can neither gain nor lose attributes); (2) life (God neither became nor is becoming; His life never began nor will it ever end); (3) moral character (God can become neither better nor worse); and (4) purpose or plan (God's decree is unalterable). We shall now consider each of these in turn.

Constancy of Being, Life, Character, and Plan

Immutability is a property which belongs to the divine essence in the sense that God can neither gain new attributes, which before He had not, nor lose those already His. There is no increase or decrease in the Divine Being. If God increases (either quantitatively or qualitatively), He was, necessarily, incomplete prior to the change. If God decreases, He is, necessarily, incomplete after the change. The Deity, then, is incapable of development either positively or negatively. He neither evolves nor devolves. His attributes, considered individually, can never be greater or less than what they are and have always been. God will

---

1. For those wishing to reconcile this with the limitations evident in the incarnate Christ during His earthly ministry, I recommend William G. T. Shedd's *Dogmatic Theology* (Minneapolis: Klock & Klock Christian Publishers, 1979), II:261–349.

never be wiser, more loving, more powerful, or holier than
He ever has been and ever must be.

This is at least implied in God's declaration to Moses: "I
am who I am" (Exod. 3:14); and is explicit in other texts:

> Every good and perfect gift is from above, coming down
> from the Father of the heavenly lights, who does not change
> like shifting shadows (James 1:17).
>
> I the Lord do not change. So you, O descendants of
> Jacob, are not destroyed (Mal. 3:6).
>
> Jesus Christ is the same yesterday and today and forever
> (Heb. 13:8).

When we talk about the immutability of God's life we are
very close to the notion of eternality or everlastingness. We
are saying that God never began to be nor will ever cease to
be. His life simply *is*. He did not come into existence (for to
become existent is a change from nothing to something),
nor will He go out of existence (for to cease existing is a
change from something to nothing). God is not young or
old: He *is*. Thus, we read:

> In the beginning you laid the foundations of the earth, and
> the heavens are the work of your hands. They will perish,
> but you remain; they all wear out like a garment. Like
> clothing you will change them and they will be discarded.
> But you remain the same, and your years will never end
> (Ps. 102:25-27).
>
> Before the mountains were born or you brought forth
> the earth and the world, from everlasting to everlasting you
> are God (Ps. 90:2; cf. 93:2).

Immutability may also be predicated of God's moral
character. He can become neither better (morally) nor
worse than what He is. If God could change (or become) in
respect to His moral character, it would be either for the
better or the worse. If for the better, it would indicate that
He had been morally imperfect or incomplete antecedent
to the time of change, and hence never God. If for the

worse, it would indicate that He is now morally less perfect or complete, i.e., subsequent to the time of change, and hence no longer God. It will not do to say that God might conceivably change from one perfect being into another equally perfect being. For one must then specify in what sense He has changed. What constitutes God as different in the second mode of being from what He was in the first? Does He have more attributes, fewer attributes, better or worse attributes? If God in the second mode of being has the same attributes (both quantitatively and qualitatively), in what sense is He different from what He was in the first mode of being?

To deny immutability to God's purpose or plan would be no less an affront to the Deity than to predicate change of His being, life, and character. There are, as I understand, only two reasons why God would ever be forced or need to alter His purpose: (1) if He lacked the necessary foresight or knowledge to anticipate any and all contingencies; or (2) assuming He had the needed foresight, He lacked the power or ability to effect what He had planned. But since, as we have previously argued, God is infinite in wisdom and knowledge, there can be no error or oversight in the *conception* of His purpose. Also, since He is infinite in power (omnipotent), there can be no failure or frustration in the *accomplishment* of His purpose.

The many and varied changes in the relationship that God sustains to His creatures, as well as the more conspicuous events of redemptive history, are not to be thought of as indicating a change in God's being or purpose. They are, rather, the execution in time of purposes eternally existing in the mind of God. For example, the abolition of the Mosaic Covenant was no change in God's will; it was, in fact, the fulfillment of His will, an eternal will which decreed change (i.e., change from the Mosaic to the New Covenant). Christ's coming and work were no makeshift action to remedy unforeseen defects in the Old Testament scheme. They were but the realization, historical and concrete, of what God had from eternity decreed. Again, we read:

"God is not a man, that he should lie, nor a son of man, that he should change his mind. Does he speak and then not act? Does he promise and not fulfill?" (Num. 23:19; cf. also 1 Sam. 15:29).

"The LORD foils the plans of the nations; he thwarts the purposes of the peoples. But the plans of the LORD stand firm forever, the purposes of his heart through all generations" (Ps. 33:10–11; cf. 110:4).

"The LORD Almighty has sworn, 'Surely, as I have planned, so it will be, and as I have purposed, so it will stand'" (Isa. 14:24).

"Remember this, fix it in mind, take it to heart, you rebels. Remember the former things, those of long ago; I am God, and there is no other; I am God, and there is none like me. I make known the end from the beginning, from ancient times, what is still to come. I say: My purpose will stand, and I will do all that I please. From the east I summon a bird of prey; from a far-off land, a man to fulfill my purpose. What I have said, that will I bring about; what I have planned, that will I do" (Isa. 46:8–11).

"Many are the plans in a man's heart, but it is the LORD'S purpose that prevails" (Prov. 19:21).

"But he stands alone, and who can oppose him? He does whatever he pleases" (Job 23:13).

"Because God wanted to make the unchanging nature of his purpose very clear to the heirs of what was promised, he confirmed it with an oath" (Heb. 6:17).

Can God Change His Mind?

No treatment of the doctrine of immutability would be complete without a discussion of the problem posed by God's alleged "repentance" (the most well-known instance of which being Jon. 3:10 and 4:2; see also Jer. 26:3; Joel 2:13; Amos 7:3). If God's plan is unalterable and He immutable, in what sense can it be said that He "changed His mind"?

Traditionally, students of Scripture have appealed to a common figure of speech known as "anthropopatheia," or "anthropopathism" (from the Greek *anthrōpos*, "man," plus *pathos*, "affection, feeling"). Thus, an anthropopathism is a figure of speech wherein certain human passions, feelings, mental activities, and so on are predicated of God. This, of course, is related to the more well-known figure of speech called "anthropomorphism" (again, from the Greek for "man" plus *morphē*, "form"), in which there are ascribed to God human body parts (e.g., eyes, mouth, nostrils, hands). Clark Pinnock believes that classical theists adopt this approach to the problem because of an extra-biblical presupposition concerning the nature of God: "The criterion employed here is simply the Greek ideal of perfection. The meaning of Scripture is not then determined from within Scripture, but on the basis of a higher standard, the requirements of adopted philosophical assumptions."[2]

I cannot speak in defense of those whom Pinnock here accuses, for the simple reason that he does not name them. But I can say with some confidence that most evangelicals appeal to anthropopathism because of what they believe Scripture explicitly teaches concerning the omniscience and immutability of God. It is the "analogy of faith," not Greek philosophical presuppositions, which governs their treatment of such problem texts. Passages such as Numbers 23:19 and the others cited earlier are unequivocal: God is *not* a man; He does *not* lie; He does *not* change His mind; He does *not* promise and then fail to fulfill. Would Pinnock have us affirm that Scripture is so blatantly self-contradictory? Given what we know of biblical authority (derived from the claims of Scripture on its

---

2. Clark Pinnock, "The Need for a Scriptural, and Therefore a Neo-Classical Theism, in *Perspectives on Evangelical Theology*, edited by Kenneth S. Kantzer and Stanley N. Gundry (Grand Rapids: Baker Book House, 1979), p. 40. See also the response to Pinnock by Richard A. Muller, "Incarnation, Immutability, and the Case for Classical Theism," *WTJ* 45 (Spring 1983):22–40.

own behalf and not from preconceived philosophical
assumptions!), are we not justified in interpreting the
unclear in the light of the clear and utilizing a figure of
speech generally acknowledged as entirely legitimate?

However, beyond even this we should note that what we
find in the case of Jonah and the Ninevites, for example, is
not an *unqualified* and *unconditional* declaration of purpose. Consider carefully the nature of this passage from
Jeremiah (18:5–12):

> "Then the word of the LORD came to me: "O house of Israel,
> can I not do with you as this potter does?" declares the
> LORD. "Like clay in the hand of the potter, so are you in my
> hand, O house of Israel. If at any time I announce that a
> nation or kingdom is to be uprooted, torn down and
> destroyed, and if that nation I warned repents of its evil,
> then I will relent and not inflict on it the disaster I had
> planned. And if at another time I announce that a nation or
> kingdom is to be built up and planted, and if it does evil in
> my sight and does not obey me, then I will reconsider the
> good I had intended to do for it.
>
> "Now therefore say to the people of Judah and those
> living in Jerusalem, 'This is what the LORD says: Look! I am
> preparing a disaster for you and devising a plan against
> you. So turn from your evil ways, each one of you, and
> reform your ways and your actions.' But they will reply, 'It's
> no use. We will continue with our own plans; each of us
> will follow the stubbornness of his evil heart.' "

That God declared His intention to destroy Nineveh, only
to withhold His hand when they repented, is thus no
threat to the doctrine of immutability. On the contrary,
had God destroyed Nineveh notwithstanding its repentance, He would have shown Himself mutable! Shedd
explains:

> If God had treated the Ninevites after their repentance, as
> he had threatened to treat them before their repentance,

this would have proved him to be mutable. It would have showed him to be at one time displeased with impenitence, and at another with penitence. Charnocke [sic] (Immutability of God) remarks that "the unchangeableness of God, when considered in relation to the exercise of his attributes in the government of the world, consists not in always acting in the same manner, however cases and circumstances may alter; but in always doing what is right, and in adapting his treatment of his intelligent creatures to the variation of their actions and characters. When the devils, now fallen, stood as glorious angels, they were the objects of God's love, necessarily; when they fell, they were the objects of God's hatred, because impure. The same reason which made him love them while they were pure, made him hate them when they were criminal." It is one thing for God to will a change in created things external to himself, and another thing for him to change in his own nature and character.[3]

All this is simply to say that God's immutability requires Him to treat the wicked differently from the righteous. When the wicked repent, His treatment of them must change. Therefore, according to Strong, God's immutability "is not that of the stone, that has no internal experience, but rather that of the column of mercury, that rises and falls with every change in the temperature of the surrounding atmosphere."[4]

We conclude, then, that it is a principle of God's immutable being (as revealed by Him in Scripture) that He punishes the wicked and recalcitrant but blesses and forgives the righteous and repentant. If God were to reveal Himself as such (as, in fact, He has done), only to punish the repentant and bless the recalcitrant, this would constitute real change and thus destroy immutability. God's declaration of intent to punish the Ninevites because of their sinful

3. Shedd, *Dogmatic Theology*, I:352–53.
4. A. H. Strong, *Systematic Theology* (Old Tappan: Fleming H. Revell, 1970), p. 258.

behavior and wickedness is based on the assumption that they are and will remain wicked. However, if and when they repent (as they did), to punish them notwithstanding would constitute a change, indeed reversal, in God's will and word, to the effect that He *now*, as over against the past, *punishes* rather than blesses the repentant.

God Is Dependable

What all this means, very simply, is that God is *dependable!* Our trust in Him is therefore a *confident* trust, for we know that He will not—indeed cannot—change. His purposes are unfailing, His promises unassailable. It is because the God who promised us eternal life is immutable that we may rest assured that nothing, not trouble or hardship or persecution or famine or nakedness or danger or sword shall separate us from the love of Christ. It is because Jesus Christ *is* the same yesterday, today, and forever that neither angels nor demons, neither the present nor the future, no not even powers, height, depth, nor anything else in all creation, will be able to separate us from the love of God that is in Christ Jesus our Lord (Rom. 8:35–39)!

8

How Sweet the Sound

Grace

Triune! Eternal! Omniscient! Omnipresent! Omnipotent! Immutable! The God of whom these things are true is indeed a great and majestic Being. Who is like unto the Lord and with whom may we compare Him? Is there another whose knowledge and power are without limit, whose life is everlasting, whose will and ways do not change, and for whom the boundaries of the universe offer no barrier? Indeed, this God is a great God!

But to say of God that He is great is not enough. For as Millard Erickson has reminded us, God, though great, "might conceivably be an immoral or amoral being, exercising his power and knowledge in a capricious or even cruel fashion."[1] No, we must proceed further in our description of the Deity; we must proceed from His greatness to His *goodness.* This God whose power and presence are illimitable, whose wisdom and will are incomparable, is a God no less abounding in love and longsuffering, mercy and grace. Therefore, although simple, yet profound is the child's dinner prayer: "God is

1. Millard Erickson, *Christian Theology* (Grand Rapids: Baker Book House, 1983), I:283–84.

117

great, God is *good*, and we thank Him for this food. Amen."

When we refer to the "goodness" of God we mean very simply that He is benevolent. God's goodness is but the inclination and resolve of His nature to promote the welfare and happiness of His creatures. This more general attribute of goodness may be manifested in the delay of penal judgment, in which case we speak of God's "long-suffering." God's goodness as manifested in the restoration of the wretched is what the Bible calls "mercy." Likewise, God's goodness as manifested toward the guilty and undeserving is referred to in Scripture as "grace." It is this latter display of the goodness of God, in which His love for the hell-deserving sinner is most keenly evident, that concerns us in this chapter.[2]

Common Grace Defined and Manifested

The verdict of the apostle Paul on the universal condition of humanity is, to say the least, a bleak one. Drawing upon the testimony of the Old Testament, he writes: "There is no one righteous, not even one; there is no one who understands, no one who seeks God. All have turned away, they have together become worthless; there is no one who does good, not even one" (Rom. 3:10–12).

Such is the predicament of man outside Christ. Theologians call it total depravity. But, as John Murray has observed, this apostolic assessment of human nature forces us to deal with a series of very insistent questions:

> How is it that men who still lie under the wrath and curse of God and are heirs of hell enjoy so many good gifts at the hand of God? How is it that men who are not savingly

2. An excellent survey of "grace" in New Testament theology is provided by Donald Guthrie, *New Testament Theology* (Downers Grove: InterVarsity Press, 1981), pp. 602–40.

renewed by the Spirit of God nevertheless exhibit so many qualities, gifts and accomplishments that promote the preservation, temporal happiness, cultural progress, social and economic improvement of themselves and of others? How is it that races and peoples that have been apparently untouched by the redemptive and regenerative influences of the gospel contribute so much to what we call human civilization? To put the question most comprehensively: how is it that this sin-cursed world enjoys so much favour and kindness at the hand of its holy and ever-blessed Creator?[3]

I believe the answer to these questions is to be found in the distinction which the Bible draws between God's common, or non-soteric, grace and His special, or soteric, grace.

The common grace of God has been variously defined. According to Charles Hodge, the Bible teaches that "the Holy Spirit as the Spirit of truth, of holiness, and of life in all its forms, is present with every human mind, enforcing truth, restraining from evil, exciting to good, and imparting wisdom or strength, when, where, and in what measure seemeth to Him good. . . . This is what in theology is called common grace."[4]

Abraham Kuyper defines common grace as "that act of God by which *negatively* He curbs the operations of Satan, death, and sin, and by which *positively* He creates an intermediate state for this cosmos, as well as for our human race, which is and continues to be deeply and radically sinful, but in which sin cannot work out its end."[5]

A simpler and more direct definition of common grace is given by John Murray. Common grace, he writes, "is every favour of whatever kind or degree, falling short of salvation,

3. John Murray, "Common Grace," in *Collected Writings of John Murray* (Edinburgh: The Banner of Truth Trust, 1977), II:93.

4. Charles Hodge, *Systematic Theology* (Grand Rapids: Wm. B. Eerdmans, 1970), II:667.

5. Abraham Kuyper, *Principles of Sacred Theology*, translated by J. Hendrik De Vries (Grand Rapids: Wm. B. Eerdmans, 1969), p. 279.

which this undeserving and sin-cursed world enjoys at the hand of God."[6] With this as a working definition we may proceed to describe the varied manifestations of common grace as they occur in both the creation and creature.

The first aspect of common grace is what we might call negative or preventative. Its essential characteristic is that of restraint. Although the restraint that God places upon sin and its effects is neither complete (else no sin would exist at all) nor uniform (else all men would be equally evil or good), it is of such a nature that the expression and effects of human depravity are not permitted to reach the maximum height of which they are capable. There are several areas wherein the notion of common grace as restraint is operative.

As already noted, God exercises restraint on the sin of man. Murray explains: "God places restraint upon the workings of human depravity and thus prevents the unholy affections and principles of men from manifesting all the potentialities inherent in them. He prevents depravity from bursting forth in all its vehemence and violence."[7]

Besides placing restraint upon the ungodly tendencies of the human heart, God freely suspends the immediate manifestation of His divine wrath due unto sin. That is to say, in common grace God not only restrains the sin of man but also the ready execution of the full measure of judgment which sin demands. This latter element of restraint is especially evident in such texts as Genesis 6:3; 1 Peter 3:20; Acts 17:30; Romans 2:4; and 2 Peter 3:9.

In addition to the manifestation of common grace in the relationship God sustains to His creatures, He also holds in

6. Murray, "Common Grace," II:96. For a stimulating treatment of the grace of God, both common and special, see Jonathan Edwards, *Treatise on Grace and other posthumously published writings including Observations on the Trinity,* edited and with an introduction by Paul Helm (Greenwood: The Attic Press, 1971), pp. 25-75.

7. Murray, "Common Grace," II:98. In this regard see Gen. 4:15; 20:6; 2 Kings 19:27–28; 2 Thess. 2:6–12.

check the destructive tendencies that are part of the curse
of sin upon nature. Murray elaborates:

> Sin introduces disintegration and disorganization in every
> realm. While it is true that only in the sphere of rationality
> does sin have meaning—it originates in mind, it develops
> in mind, it resides in mind—yet sin works out disastrous
> effects outside the sphere of the rational and moral as well
> as within it. God places restraint upon these effects, he
> prevents the full development of this disintegration. He
> brings to bear upon this world in all its spheres correcting
> and preserving influences so that the ravages of sin might
> not be allowed to work out the full measure of their
> destructive power.[8]

The second aspect of common grace is more positive in
thrust. God not only restrains the sinful operations and
effects of the human heart, He also bestows upon both
nature and humanity manifold blessings both physical
and spiritual. These blessings, however, fall short of redemption itself.

The grace of God displayed throughout the created
order is marvelous indeed:

> You care for the land and water it; you enrich it abundantly.
> The streams of God are filled with water to provide the
> people with grain, for so you have ordained it. You drench
> its furrows and level its ridges; you soften it with showers
> and bless its crops. You crown the year with your bounty,
> and your carts overflow with abundance. The grasslands of
> the desert overflow; the hills are clothed with gladness. The
> meadows are covered with flocks and the valleys are
> mantled with grain; they shout for joy and sing (Ps.
> 65:9–13).

Similar descriptions may be found in Psalm 104:10–30;
145:1–16; and 136:25.

---

8. Ibid., II:101. In this regard see Gen. 3:17 and 9:2–5.

Furthermore, God not only restrains evil in unredeemed men but also endows them, Murray continues, with

> gifts, talents, and aptitudes; he stimulates them with interest and purpose to the practice of virtues, the pursuance of worthy tasks, and the cultivation of arts and sciences that occupy the time, activity and energy of men and that make for the benefit and civilization of the human race. He ordains institutions for the protection and promotion of right, the preservation of liberty, the advance of knowledge and the improvement of physical and moral conditions. We may regard these interests, pursuits and institutions as exercising both an expulsive and impulsive influence. Occupying the energy, activity and time of men they prevent the indulgence of less noble and ignoble pursuits and they exercise an ameliorating, moralizing, stabilizing and civilizing influence upon the social organism.[9]

Of this manifestation of common grace we read in Genesis 39:5; Acts 14:16–17; Matthew 5:44–45; Luke 6:35–36; 16:25. It is because of such operations of common grace that the unregenerate may be said to perform "good" (cf. 2 Kings 10:30; 12:2; Matt. 5:46; Luke 6:33; Rom. 2:14–15). However, Murray adds, "the good attributed to unregenerate men is after all only relative good. It is not good in the sense of meeting in motivation, principle and aim the requirements of God's law and the demands of his holiness,"[10] and thus can in no way commend them to the righteousness of the Father. We must never lose sight of the fact that all such operations of "grace" (so-called because undeserved) are *non-saving*, being neither in design nor effect such as would produce new life in Christ.

Finally, we may say that whereas the ultimate purpose of common grace is the glory of God, its more immediate

9. Ibid., II:102–03. The institutions here in mind include primarily (but not exclusively) the family and the state (1 Peter 2:14; Rom. 13:1–4; 1 Tim. 2:1–2).
10. Ibid., II:107.

design is to serve the aims and interests of saving grace. In other words, says Murray,

> it is that sphere of life or broad stream of history provided by common grace that provides the sphere of operation for God's special purpose of redemption and salvation. This simply means that this world upheld and preserved by God's grace is the sphere and platform upon which supervene the operations of special grace and in which special grace works to the accomplishment of his saving purpose and the perfection of the whole body of the elect.[11]

Soteric Grace for the Elect

The elect of God are recipients not only of all the benefits of common grace, but also of *special* grace. In fact, it is precisely the bestowal of special grace which constitutes them as the "elect" as over against those from whom it is withheld, namely, the "non-elect." Special grace is, of course, *saving* grace, and thus contrary to common grace *does* have as its design and effect the bestowal of eternal life through faith in Jesus Christ.

Herman Bavinck defined the special or soteric grace of God in this way: "Ascribed to God, grace is his voluntary, unrestrained, unmerited favor toward guilty sinners, granting them justification and life instead of the penalty of death, which they deserved."[12]

Berkhof defined it simply as "the free bestowal of kindness on one who has no claim to it."[13] Packer ex-

11. Ibid., II:113. Yet another secondary purpose of common grace is to provide a means by which recipients of special grace may fulfill the cultural mandate. In addition, according to Carl Henry in *God, Revelation and Authority* (Waco: Word Books, 1982), VI:457, God "preserves rebellious humanity [through common grace] in order to call it to contrition and to apprise it of the approaching assize of men and nations."

12. Herman Bavinck, *The Doctrine of God*, translated, edited and outlined by William Hendriksen (Edinburgh: The Banner of Truth Trust, 1977), p. 208.

13. Louis Berkhof, *Systematic Theology* (Grand Rapids: Wm. B. Eerdmans, 1972), p. 71.

pressed it in this way: "The grace of God is love freely shown towards guilty sinners, contrary to their merit and indeed in defiance of their demerit. It is God showing goodness to persons who deserve only severity, and had no reason to expect anything but severity."[14]

As one might expect, the doctrine of God's grace is a vast and multifaceted subject. Because of this, I have chosen to focus in on ten principles or characteristics relating to the special grace of God, especially as it is found in the Pauline literature.

1. The first and possibly most fundamental characteristic of divine grace is that it presupposes sin and guilt. Grace has meaning *only* when men are seen as fallen, unworthy of salvation, and liable to eternal wrath. It is precisely because people today have lost sight of the depths of human depravity that they think so little of divine grace. What makes Paul's declaration that we are saved "by grace" so significant is his earlier declaration that we were "dead" in trespasses and sins, "gratifying the cravings of our sinful nature," "following its desires and thoughts," and were by nature the children of divine wrath (Eph. 2:1–10).

2. Grace does not contemplate sinners merely as *unde-serving*, but as *ill*-deserving. So often we are inclined to think of ourselves prior to our salvation as in some sense "neutral" in the sight of God. We are willing to admit that we have done nothing to deserve His favor. Our works, regardless of their character, are unacceptable in His glorious presence. But this is entirely insufficient as a background to the understanding of divine grace. It is not simply that we do not deserve grace: we *do* deserve hell! Fallen and unredeemed humanity is not to be conceived as merely helpless, but as openly and vehemently *hostile* toward God. It is one thing to be without a God-approved righteousness. It is altogether another thing to be wholly

*un*righteous and thus the object of divine wrath. It is, then, against the background of having been at one time the *enemies* of God that divine grace is to be portrayed (Rom. 5:10).

3. Furthermore, grace is not to be thought of as in any sense dependent upon the merit or demerit of its objects. This may be expressed in two ways. First, grace ceases to be grace if God is compelled to bestow it in the presence of human merit. According to Lewis Chafer:

> If God should discover the least degree of merit in the sinner, this, in strict righteousness, He must recognize and duly acknowledge. By such a recognition of human merit, He would be discharging an obligation toward the sinner and the discharge of that obligation toward the sinner would be the payment, or recognition, of a debt.[15]

Second, grace ceases to be grace if God is compelled to withdraw it in the presence of human demerit. Indeed, grace is seen to be infinitely glorious only when it operates, as Packer says, "in defiance of" human demerit! Therefore, grace is *not* treating a person less than, as, or greater than he deserves. It is treating a person without the slightest reference to desert whatsoever, but solely according to the infinite goodness and sovereign purpose of God.

4. Grace cannot incur a debt, which is to say that it is unrecompensed. Since grace is a gift, no work is to be performed, no offering made, with a view to *repaying* God for His favor. The biblical response to grace received is service and obedience that spring not from a sense of legal obligation, but from a heart overwhelmed by love and stirred by gratitude.

5. In respect to justification, grace stands opposed to works (Rom. 4:4–5; 11:6). However, in respect to sanctification, grace is the source of works. This simply means that

15. Lewis Sperry Chafer, *Grace* (Grand Rapids: Zondervan, 1972), p. 8.

whereas we are saved by grace and *not* of works, we *are* saved by grace *unto* good works. Good works are the fruit, not the root, of God's saving grace (see esp. Eph. 2:8–10).

6. It thus comes as no surprise that in Scripture grace and salvation stand together as cause is related to effect. It is the grace of God which "brings" salvation (Titus 2:11). We are saved by grace through faith (Eph. 2:8–9).

7. This grace that saves is *eternal*, but is manifested in the historical appearance of Christ. Paul speaks of the power of God by which we have been saved and called to holiness, "not because of anything we have done but because of his own purpose and grace. This grace was given us in Christ Jesus before the beginning of time, but it has now been revealed through the appearing of our Savior, Christ Jesus, who has destroyed death and has brought life and immortality to light through the gospel" (2 Tim. 1:9–10).

8. Moreover, this grace is free! Just think of it—free grace! But, of course, if grace were not free it would not be grace. True indeed, but what a glorious tautology it is: ". . . justified freely by his grace through the redemption that came by Christ Jesus[!]" (Rom. 3:24).

9. Grace is also sovereign. That is to say, it is optional in its exercise and extent. Although God *is* gracious in His eternal being, He need not *be* gracious or shower His grace upon anyone. If grace were at any time an *obligation* of God, it would cease to be grace. God's grace, therefore, is distinguishing. He graciously saves some but not all, not based on anything present in the creature either possible or actual, foreseen or foreordained, but wholly according to His sovereign good pleasure.

10. Finally, grace is described in Scripture as the foundation or the means of, among other things, our election (Rom. 11:5), our regeneration (Eph. 2:5; Titus 3:5–7), our redemption (2 Cor. 8:9; Eph. 1:7), our justification (Rom. 3:24; Titus 3:5–7), indeed, the whole of our salvation (Eph. 2:8).

What, then, can we say, but that after these many centuries, through these many toils and trials—GRACE IS STILL AMAZING!

A Supplementary Note

The grace of God which has engaged our attention is more than an attitude or disposition in the divine nature. It *is* surely that, but an examination of the usage of this word in Scripture reveals that "grace," if thought of only as an abstract and static principle, is deprived of its deeper implications.

The grace of God, for example, is the power of God's Spirit converting the soul. It is the activity or movement of God whereby He saves and justifies the individual through faith (see esp. Rom. 3:24; 5:15, 17). Therefore, grace is not something in which we merely believe; it is something we experience as well.

Grace, however, is not only the divine act by which God initiates our spiritual life, but also the very power by which we are sustained in, nourished, and proceed through that life. The energizing and sanctifying work of the indwelling Spirit *is* the grace of God. After Paul had prayed three times for God to deliver him from his thorn in the flesh, he received this answer: "My grace is sufficient for you, for my power is made perfect in weakness" (2 Cor. 12:9).

Although Paul undoubtedly derived encouragement and strength to face his daily trials by reflecting on the magnificence of God's unmerited favor, in this text he appears to speak rather of an experiential reality of a more dynamic nature. It is the operative power of the indwelling Spirit to which Paul refers. *That* is the grace of God.

We should also consider in this regard the many references to the grace of God in Paul's opening greetings and concluding benedictions (Rom. 1:7; 1 Cor. 1:3; 2 Cor. 1:3; Gal. 1:3; Eph. 1:2; Phil. 1:2; Col. 1:2; 1 Thess. 1:1; 2 Thess. 1:2; Titus 1:4; 2 Cor. 13:14). This no mere literary formality, but an earnest and constant wish of Paul that his converts may continue to experience grace, that they may know afresh the gracious power of God moving in their lives, that they may find in that grace the spiritual resources by which to live in a way pleasing to Him.

Besides the general soteriological usage of the word with which everyone is familiar, "grace" can also denote the particular acts of God whereby He grants enablement for some service or authorization for a specific duty or mission (Rom. 12:3; 15:15–16; 1 Cor. 3:10). It is not without significance that the word *grace* and its derivatives are used in the description of what we call "spiritual gifts." We read in Romans 12:6: "We have different gifts [*charismata*], according to the grace [*charin*] given us."

Finally, the word *grace* is used in a variety of ways in the course of Paul's discussion of Christian stewardship (2 Cor. 8–9). It is used with reference to the supernatural *enablement* bestowed by God, as a result of which one gives despite poverty (2 Cor. 8:1, 9). It refers to the *ministry* of giving (2 Cor. 8:6, 7, 19), the *privilege* of giving (2 Cor. 8:4), and even to the *gift* itself (1 Cor. 16:3).[16]

16. See also James D. G. Dunn, *Jesus and the Spirit* (Philadelphia: The Westminster Press, 1975), pp. 202–05.

9

John 3:16—Just What *Does* It Mean?

Love

The love of God, as with His grace, mercy, and longsuffering, is another aspect of that more general attribute which we have referred to as "goodness." The love of God, however, is not merely an attribute which He displays: love is something God *is*. The apostle John concludes that lovelessness on the part of the individual is an indication that one does not know God, "because God is love" (1 John 4:8). Love, therefore, according to Carl Henry, "is not accidental or incidental to God; it is an essential revelation of the divine nature, a fundamental and eternal perfection."[1]

But what is love? Love is simply the communication by God *of Himself* to His creatures. It is the benevolent disposition or inclination in God that impels to the bestowing of benefits both physical and spiritual upon those created in His image (and is thus in this respect synonymous with grace). However, insofar as not all of God's creatures receive and experience His love in precisely the

---

1. Carl F. H. Henry, *God, Revelation and Authority* (Waco: Word Books, 1982), VI:341.

same manner or to the same degree, one cannot speak of "the love of God" without qualification. It seems inescapable, both from Scripture and experience, that we differentiate between the love of God as manifested in common grace and the love of God as manifested in special grace (see chapter eight).

The love of God as manifested in common grace is the love of God as *creator*, which consists of providential kindness, mercy, and longsuffering. It is an indiscriminate and universal love which constrains to the bestowing of all physical and spiritual benefits excepting that of salvation. It is received and experienced by the elect and non-elect alike (see Matt. 5:43–48; Luke 6:27–38).[2]

The love of God as manifested in special grace is the love of God as *savior*, which consists of redemption, the efficacy of regenerating grace, and the irrevocable possession of eternal life. It is a discriminate and particular love that constrains to the bestowing of the grace of eternal life in Christ. It is received and experienced by the elect only.

The Principles of Divine Love

In our study of divine grace I outlined some ten principles or characteristics of that attribute. The teaching of Scripture concerning divine love is no less extensive.[3] Witness the following twelve points:

1. Like grace, the saving love of God is undeserved. This is but to say that the love of God for sinners, which issues in their salvation, finds no obstacle in their sin. God loves

2. See the discussion of these texts by John Murray, "The Atonement and the Free Offer of the Gospel," in *Collected Writings of John Murray* (Edinburgh: The Banner of Truth Trust, 1976), I:65–68.

3. For a more complete treatment of "love" in Scripture, both divine and human, see Leon Morris, *Testaments of Love: A Study of Love in the Bible* (Grand Rapids: Wm. B. Eerdmans, 1981).

us while we are *yet* sinners precisely in order that the glory
of His love might be supremely magnified. It was when we
were still "powerless" that "Christ died for the ungodly"
(Rom. 5:6). Again, Paul stresses that "God demonstrates his
own love for us in this: While we were still sinners, Christ
died for us" (Rom. 5:8; cf. Deut. 7:6–8). Consequently, the
sole cause of God's saving love for sinners is *God Himself!*

> "What was there in me that could merit esteem,
>   Or give the Creator delight?
> 'Twas even so, Father, I ever must sing,
>   Because it seemed good in Thy sight."[4]

2. This love of God, then, is clearly the source or cause of
the atoning work of Christ. God does not love men because
Christ died for them. Christ died for them because God
loved them. The death of the Savior is not to be conceived
as restoring in men something on the basis of which we
might then win God's love. The sacrifice of Christ does not
procure God's affection, as if it were necessary, through
His sufferings, to extract love from an otherwise stern,
unwilling, reluctant Deity. On the contrary, God's love
constrains to the death of Christ and is supremely manifested therein. In a word, the saving love of God is *giving:*

"I have been crucified with Christ and I no longer live,
but Christ lives in me. The life I live in the body, I live by
faith in the Son of God, *who loved me and gave himself* for
me" (Gal. 2:20, *emphasis mine).*

"This is how God *showed* his love among us: He *sent* his
one and only Son into the world that we might live through
him. This is love: not that we loved God, but that he loved
us and *sent* his Son as an atoning sacrifice for our sins"
(1 John 4:9–10, *emphasis mine).*

"For God so loved the world that he *gave* his one and

---

4. Morris concludes that the love of God for the undeserving is, in fact, the
"one great overriding theme" of the Bible's teaching on the subject (ibid., p. 271).

only Son, that whoever believes in him shall not perish but have eternal life" (John 3:16, *emphasis mine*).

"Be imitators of God, therefore, as dearly loved children and live a life of love, just as Christ loved us and *gave himself* up for us as a fragrant offering and sacrifice to God" (Eph. 5:1–2, *emphasis mine*).

"Husbands, love your wives, just as Christ loved the church and *gave himself* up for her" (Eph. 5:25, *emphasis mine*).

The citation of such texts could continue seemingly without end (see also Rom. 5:6–8; 1 John 3:16; Rev. 1:5). But after a survey of only these few it is evident that, in the words of Henry, "almost invariably the New Testament Epistles expound God's love for us by reference to the cross. To eliminate the death of Christ for sinners would eviscerate the very heart of divine love as portrayed in the New Testament."[5]

3. The saving love of God is also sovereign. John Murray explains as follows:

> Truly God is love. Love is not something adventitious; it is not something that God may choose to be or choose not to be. He *is* love, and that necessarily, inherently, and eternally. As God is spirit, as he is light, so he is love. Yet it belongs to the very essence of electing love to recognize that it is not inherently necessary to that love which God necessarily and eternally is that he should set such love as issues in redemption and adoption upon utterly undesirable and hell-deserving objects. It was of the free and sovereign good pleasure of his will, a good pleasure that emanated from the depths of his own goodness, that he chose a people to be heirs of God and joint-heirs with Christ. The reason resides wholly in himself and proceeds from determinations that are peculiarly his as the "I am that I am."[6]

5. Henry, *God, Revelation and Authority*, VI:355.
6. John Murray, *Redemption: Accomplished and Applied* (Grand Rapids: Wm. B. Eerdmans, 1978), p. 10.

A. W. Pink concurs. Concerning the statement, "Jacob have I loved but Esau have I hated," he writes:

> There was no more reason in Jacob why he should be the object of Divine love, than there was in Esau. They both had the same parents, and were born at the same time, being twins [neither one had done anything good or evil]: yet God loved the one and hated the other! Why? Because it pleased Him to do so.[7]

Thus, to say that love is sovereign is to say it is distinguishing. It is, by definition as *saving* love, bestowed upon and experienced by those only who are in fact *saved* (i.e., the elect). Although there is surely a sense in which God loves the non-elect, He does *not* love them redemptively. If He did, they would certainly be redeemed. God loves them, but *not* savingly, else they would certainly be saved. All this is but to say that God's eternal, *electing* love is not universal but particular. In this regard we should take note of the implications vis-á-vis the extent of the atonement. Gary Long explains:

> To say that Christ's sacrificial death, which is the highest expression of divine love to men, applies equally to all men and then observe that a multitude of mankind has and is entering a Christless eternity certainly does not magnify God's love or His wisdom. Will God love those who are in hell equally with the redeemed who are with Christ in eternity? Certainly not, for a love of this nature cannot be that love of God which is immutable and eternal. What kind of God is it who delivers up His Son to die for the redemption of each and every individual of mankind, yet does not send multitudes the gospel to acquaint them with

7. A. W. Pink, *The Attributes of God* (Grand Rapids: Baker Book House, n.d.), p. 93. For those interested in further study of this text and the relationship of God's love to the elect and non-elect, I recommend the technical but unsurpassed study of John Piper, *The Justification of God: An Exegetical and Theological Study of Romans 9:1–23* (Grand Rapids: Baker Book House, 1983).

the gift of salvation, or sends [sic] them His Spirit to apply
the benefit of redemption, or gives [sic] them saving faith to
lay hold upon it? Such a love would be unworthy of God
and a mockery to the very persons who, according to the
theory of universal redemption, were bought with Christ's
blood. In effect, the universal redemptionist's view reduces
to this: God loved each and every one enough to have
Christ die for them, but He did not love them enough to
save them, or for that matter, enough to pray for them (cf.
John 17:9).[8]

4. It is also to the saving love of God that we trace the
cause of our predestination. Paul writes: "For those God
foreknew he also predestined to be conformed to the
likeness of his Son, that he might be the firstborn among
many brothers" (Rom. 8:29).

Although God certainly foresees all that comes to pass
(see chapter four), more than bare foresight is envisioned
here. The foreknowledge of which Paul speaks in Romans
8:29 is manifestly distinguishing, not universal: it is a
foreknowledge of those and those only who are in turn
predestined, called, justified, and glorified. The suggestion
that God's foreknowledge has for its object the faith of man
founders on five crucial considerations. First, the text
simply does not refer to "faith" as the object of God's
foresight. The "faith" of man must be imported from
without, for it is conspicuously absent from the text itself.
"It should be observed," notes Murray, "that the text says
'whom he foreknew'; whom is the object of the verb and
there is no qualifying addition. This, of itself, shows that,
unless there is some other compelling reason, the expression 'whom he foreknew' contains within itself the differentiation which is presupposed."[9] More on this below.

8. Gary D. Long, Definite Atonement (Nutley: Presbyterian and Reformed
Publishing, 1976), p. 9. On the distinguishing love of God, see also Eph. 1:5; 2:4;
5:25; Rev. 3:9; Rom. 9:13; Col. 3:12; 1 Thess. 1:4; 2 Thess. 2:13; 1 John 3:1.
9. John Murray, The Epistle to the Romans (Grand Rapids: Wm. B. Eerdmans,
1971), 1:316–17.

Second, this suggestion assumes what the Bible elsewhere clearly denies, namely, that man of his own free will
is capable of saving faith, (see John 1:12–13; 3:3–8; 6:37–46;
Rom. 3:10–18; 8:5–8; 9:14–24; 1 Cor. 2:14; 2 Cor. 4:1–6; Eph.
2:1–10; 4:17–19; Phil. 1:29; 2 Tim. 2:25).

Third, if we adopt this interpretation, the Christian
would certainly have something of which to boast. God
would of necessity be obligated to share His glory with
him who of his own free will saw fit to embrace the
provision of Christ's death.

Fourth, the notion that God's predestinating purpose is
conditioned upon man's free-will faith contravenes the
divine monergism which characterizes the entire para-
graph. It is *God* who foreknows, *God* who predestines, *God*
who calls, *God* who justifies, *God* who glorifies, and *God*
who preserves (vv. 31–39).

Fifth, and finally, even if it were granted that "foreknew" means the foresight of faith, Murray points out
that

the biblical doctrine of sovereign election is not thereby
eliminated or disproven. For it is certainly true that God
foresees faith; he foresees all that comes to pass. The
question would then simply be: whence proceeds this faith
which God foresees? And the only biblical answer is that
the faith which God foresees is the faith he himself creates
(cf. John 3:3–8; 6:44, 45, 65; Eph. 2:8; Phil. 1:29; II Peter 1:2).[10]

Clearly, then, the notion of a barren foresight or mere
prevision does not adequately explain the apostle's
thought. Murray's explanation is far more preferable:

Many times in Scripture "know" has a pregnant meaning
which goes beyond that of mere cognition. It is used in a
sense practically synonymous with "love," to set regard

10. Ibid., I:316.

upon, to know with peculiar interest, delight, affection, and
action (cf. Gen. 18:19; Exod. 2:25; Psalm 1:6; 144:3; Jer. 1:5;
Amos 3:2; Hosea 13:5; Matt. 7:23; I Cor. 8:3; Gal. 4:9; II Tim.
2:19; I John 3:1). There is no reason why this import of the
word "know" should not be applied to "foreknow" in this
passage, as also in 11:2 where it also occurs in the same
kind of construction and where the thought of election is
patently present (cf. 11: 5, 6). When this import is appreciated, then there is no reason for adding any qualifying notion
and "whom he foreknew" is seen to contain within itself
the differentiating element required. It means "whom he
set regard upon" or "whom he knew from eternity with
distinguishing affection and delight" and is virtually equivalent to "whom he foreloved".[11]

It is, therefore, God's eternal and distinguishing *love*,
conditioned upon no other grounds than His own sovereign and immutable purpose, that explains and accounts
for our predestination unto conformity to Christ.

5. This same love of God is the reason for our adoption
as sons. It was "in love" that God "predestined us to be
adopted as his sons through Jesus Christ, in accordance
[not with our foreseen faith but *in accordance*] with his
pleasure and will" (Eph. 1:4b–5). It is because God loved
that he predestinated. So, again, writes Murray,

it is impossible to think of this love as exercised toward
those not predestinated to adoption. The love impelling to
predestination is of such a *character* that the determinate
issue in adoption flows from it; everything hangs on the
qualitative distinctiveness of the love involved. The parallel-
ism in verses 4 and 5 adds force to the particularism of both
the love and its issue. Verse 4 speaks of election in Christ
before the foundation of the world as directed to the end
that the elect should be holy and without blemish, verse 5

11. Ibid., I:317.

of love as directed to adoption. The distinguishing quality of the love corresponds to the distinguishing quality of the election.[12]

"How great is the love the Father has lavished on us," John understandably exclaims, "that we should be called children of God" (1 John 3:1)!

> Behold the amazing gift of love
> The Father hath bestowed,
> On us the sinful sons of men,
> To call us sons of God! [Isaac Watts]

6. We should not in the least be surprised that this love of God is described as "great." It was because of his "great love for us" that God made us alive together with Christ. It is a great love because it can never be exhausted, its depths never plumbed, its purpose never thwarted by the sin of man (Eph. 2:4–5). And again, the context will not permit this love to be universalized. Murray writes that it is a love

> which impels to the efficacious actions [of being quickened together with Christ and raised with Him] and cannot have an extent broader than those embraced in the actions specified. The same kind of relationship obtains between the "great love" and the saving actions as obtains between love and predestination in Ephesians 1:5 and, again, the quality of the love must be as distinctive as the saving acts which are its result.[13]

7. The saving love of God is eternal. It was "before the creation of the world" (Eph. 1:4–5) that He chose us in Christ and predestined us unto adoption as sons (cf. 2 Thess. 2:13). Charles Spurgeon elaborates:

12. Murray, "The Atonement and the Free Offer of the Gospel," I:70–71.
13. Ibid., I:71.

In the very beginning, when this great universe lay in the
mind of God, like unborn forests in the acorn cup; long ere
the echoes awoke the solitudes; before the mountains were
brought forth; and long ere the light flashed through the
sky, God loved His chosen creatures. Before there was any
created being—when the ether was not fanned by an
angel's wing, when space itself had not an existence, where
there was nothing save God alone—even then, in that
loneliness of Deity, and in that deep quiet and profundity,
His bowels moved with love for His chosen. Their names
were written on His heart, and then were they dear to His
soul. Jesus loved His people before the foundation of the
world—even from eternity! and when He called me by His
grace, He said to me, "I have loved *thee* with an everlasting
love: therefore with lovingkindness have I drawn thee."[14]

8. This love is not only eternal in its conception, it is
irrevocable in its purpose. "Who shall separate us from the
love of Christ? Shall trouble or hardship or persecution or
famine or nakedness or danger or sword?" (Rom. 8:35).
Nothing, Paul insists and assures, shall be able to separate
us from the love of Christ. That alone can sever us from the
embrace of God's love which is greater than God. Hence we
rest secure.

> My name from the palms of His hands
>   Eternity will not erase;
> Impress'd on His heart it remains,
>   In marks of indelible grace.

9. In Romans 5, Paul can speak of a *confident* hope on no
other ground than that God has loved us in Christ. It is
because He loved us when we were yet His enemies, a love
demonstrated by the sending of His Son, that His love for
us now that we are His friends is unshakeable. This "much

14. Charles H. Spurgeon, *C. H. Spurgeon Autobiography, Volume I: The Early
Years 1834–1859* (Edinburgh: The Banner of Truth Trust, 1973), p. 167.

more" argument of Romans 5:6–11 is encouragement indeed. Paul says, in effect, that if when we were alienated from God He, notwithstanding, reconciled us to Himself through His Son, *how much more*, now that we have been graciously instated in His favor and the alienation removed, shall the exalted and everlasting life of Christ insure our being saved to the uttermost! Murray comments: "It would be a violation of the wisdom, goodness, and faithfulness of God to suppose that he would have done the greater [love His enemies] and fail in the lesser [love His friends]."[15]

10. Discipline, no less than life, is a product of the divine love: "My son, do not make light of the Lord's discipline, and do not lose heart when he rebukes you, because the Lord disciplines those he loves, and he punishes everyone he accepts as a son" (Heb. 12:5b–6).

The Hebrew Christians to whom these words were addressed had mistakenly come to think that the absence of affliction was a sign of God's special favor and, therefore, that suffering and oppression were an indication of His displeasure. On the contrary, so far from being a proof of God's anger or rejection of us, afflictions are evidence of His fatherly love. Discipline, writes Philip Hughes, "is the mark not of a harsh and heartless father but of a father who is deeply and lovingly concerned for the well-being of his son."[16]

11. The eternal and irrevocable love which God has for His chosen also secures far more than merely the reconciliation of estranged sinners. This manifold design of God's saving love is especially evident in John's First Epistle. For example, the love that God has for us is said to make possible our love for one another. Following his discussion of God's love as witnessed in the atoning sacrifice of His

---

15. Murray, *The Epistle to the Romans*, I:175.

16. Philip Edgcumbe Hughes, *A Commentary on the Epistle to the Hebrews* (Grand Rapids: Wm. B. Eerdmans, 1977), p. 528.

Son (1 John 4:7–11), John writes: "No one has ever seen God; but if we love each other, God lives in us and his love is made complete in us" (1 John 4:12).

Other texts of Scripture confirm that God has never been seen (cf. 1 Tim. 1:17; 6:16; Exod. 33:20). How, then, can He be known? In John 1:18 the answer is given: "No one has ever seen God, but God the only Son, who is at the Father's side, has made him known."

This is all well and good, but for what purpose does John include it in this context? Evidently, according to John Stott, he wishes to say that the unseen God, revealed once in His Son, "is now revealed in His people if and when they love one another. God's love is seen in their love because their love is His love imparted to them by His Spirit."[17] The point is that although God cannot be seen in Himself, He *can* be seen in those in whom He abides when they love others with that very love wherewith they were loved! The fullness of God's redemptive love for us in Christ thus attains its intended goal in *our love for one another.*

This notion that God's love has for its ultimate design more than the salvation of those on whom it is showered is seen yet again in 1 John 2:5. Here we read that "if anyone obeys his word, God's love is truly made complete in him." That is to say, the love of God achieves its ordained purpose when we as the recipients thereof in turn obey Him from whom it has come forth.

John pursues this same theme from yet another angle in 1 John 4:17. "Love is made complete among us," he argues, "so that we will have confidence on the day of judgment, because in this world we are like him." Once more, God's love secures its end to the degree that we who are its objects cease to fear the day of judgment. The knowledge

17. John R. W. Stott, *The Epistles of John: An Introduction and Commentary* (Grand Rapids: Wm. B. Eerdmans, 1976), p. 164.

of God's fatherly love should forever dispel any apprehension of standing in His presence. This is not presumption, but a Spirit-induced conviction that God's love has efficaciously and eternally provided for us in Christ that righteousness on the basis of which we are delivered from all penal liability. God's perfect love for us, when rightly perceived, does indeed cast out fear!

12. No wonder, then, in light of what we have seen, that Paul speaks of the love of God as incomprehensible! And yet he prays specifically that we might *know* this love that "surpasses knowledge" (Eph. 3:19). John Eadie says it beautifully. God's love

> may be known in some features and to some extent, but at the same time it stretches away into infinitude, far beyond the ken of human discovery and analysis. As a fact manifested in time and embodied in the incarnation, life, teaching, and death of the Son of God, it may be understood, for it assumed a nature of clay, bled on the cross, and lay prostrate in the tomb; but in its unbeginning existence as an eternal passion, antedating alike the Creation and the Fall, it "passeth knowledge." In the blessings which it confers—the pardon, grace, and glory which it provides—it may be seen in palpable exhibition, and experienced in happy consciousness; but in its limitless power and endless resources it baffles thought and description. In the terrible sufferings and death to which it led, and in the self-denial and sacrifices which it involved, it may be known so far by the application of human instincts and analogies; but the fathomless fervour of a Divine affection surpasses the measurements of created intellect. As the attachment of a man, it may be gauged; but as the love of a God, who can by searching find it out? Uncaused itself, it originated salvation; unresponded to amidst the "contradiction of sinners," it neither pined nor collapsed. It led from Divine immortality to human agonies and dissolution, for the victim was bound to the cross not by the nails of the military executioner, but by the "cords of love." It

loved repulsive unloveliness, and, unnourished by recipro-
cated attachment, its ardour was unquenched, nay, is
unquenchable, for it is changeless as the bosom in which it
dwells.[18]

The Immeasurable Love

No discussion of the love of God would be complete
without some statement on John 3:16. Indeed, as the title
to this chapter implies, the preceding analysis was in large
measure designed to enable us to interpret correctly and
appreciate more deeply the sense of divine love as found
in John 3:16.

The meaning of this text has frequently been obscured
by interpreters who, unfortunately, have failed to place it
in the broader context of what Scripture as a whole says
concerning this divine attribute. Therefore, in the light of
what we have already seen to be true of the love of God, let
us consider this most famous of texts.

Often the interpretation of John 3:16 begins with the
term *world*, for it is believed that herein lies the key to a
proper appreciation of the dimensions of divine love. Just
think, we are told, of the multitudes of men and women
who have, do now, and yet shall swarm across the face of
the earth. God loves them all, each and every one. Indeed,
God so loves them that He gave His only begotten Son to
die for each and every one of them. O how great the love of
God must be to embrace within its arms these uncounted
multitudes of people.

Is this what John (or Jesus, as recorded by John) had in
mind? It is undeniably his purpose to set before us the
immeasurable love of God. But are we able to perceive how
immeasurable God's love is by *measuring* how big the
world is? I think not. What is the finite sum of mankind

18. John Eadie, *Commentary on the Epistle to the Ephesians* (Minneapolis:
James and Klock Christian Publishing, 1977), pp. 257–58.

when set opposite the infinitude of God? We could as well measure the strength of the blacksmith by declaring him capable of supporting a feather on an outstretched palm! The primary force of this text is certainly to magnify the infinite quality and majesty of God's love. But such an end can never be reached by computing the extent or number of its objects. Do we to any degree heighten the value of Christ's death by ascertaining the quantity of those for whom He died? Of course not! Had He but died for one sinner, the value of His sacrifice would be not less glorious than had He suffered for ten millions of worlds!

Rather, let us pause to consider the contrast which the apostle intends for us to see. John surely desires that we reflect in our hearts upon the immeasurable character of so great a love, and that we do so by placing in contrast, one over against the other—*God* and the *world.* What does this reveal? Of what do we think concerning God when He is seen loving the world? And of what do we think concerning the world when it is seen as the object of God's love? Is the contrast this: that God is *one* and the world *many?* Is it that His love is magnified because He, as one, has loved the world, comprised of many? Again, certainly not. This love is infinitely majestic because God, as HOLY, has loved the world, as SINFUL! What strikes us is that God who is RIGHTEOUS loves the world which is UNRIGHTEOUS. This text takes root in our hearts because it declares that He who dwells in unapproachable LIGHT has deigned to enter the realm of DARKNESS; that He who is JUST has given Himself for the UNJUST (1 Peter 3:18); that He who is altogether GLORIOUS and DESIRABLE has suffered endless shame for DETESTABLE and REPUGNANT creatures, who apart from His grace respond only with hell-deserving hostility! Thus, as Murray has said,

> it is what God loved in respect of its *character* that throws into relief the incomparable and incomprehensible love of

God. To find anything else as the governing thought would detract from the emphasis. *God loved what is the antithesis of himself;* this is its marvel and greatness.[19]

When we read John's Gospel (and Epistles), we discover that the "world" is viewed fundamentally neither as the elect nor non-elect but as a collective organism: sinful, estranged, alienated from God, abiding under His wrath and curse. The world is detestable because it is the contradiction of all that is holy, good, righteous, and true. The world, then, is the contradiction of God. It is synonymous with all that is evil and noisome. It is that system of fallen humanity viewed *not* in terms of its *size* but as a satanically controlled kingdom hostile to the kingdom of Christ. It is what God loved in respect of its *quality*, therefore, *not quantity*, that sheds such glorious light on this divine attribute.

In summary, I urge that the reader carefully attend to the words of B. B. Warfield:

> The marvel . . . which the text brings before us is just that marvel above all other marvels in this marvelous world of ours—the marvel of God's love for sinners. And this is the measure by which we are invited to measure the greatness of the love of God. It is not that it is so great that it is able to extend over the whole of a big world; it is so great that it is able to prevail over the Holy God's hatred and abhorrence of sin. For herein is love, that *God* could love the *world*—the world that lies in the evil one: that God who is all-holy and just and good, could so love this world that He gave His only begotten Son for it,—that He might not judge it, but that it might be saved.[20]

19. Murray, "The Atonement and the Free Offer of the Gospel," I:79. *Emphasis mine.*

20 Benjamin Breckinridge Warfield, "God's Immeasurable Love," in *Biblical and Theological Studies,* edited by Samuel G. Craig (Philadelphia: Presbyterian and Reformed Publishing, 1952), pp. 515–16.

Warfield therefore believes that the key to the passage lies in the significance of the term *world*. He defines it as follows:

> It is not here a term of extension so much as a term of intensity. Its primary connotation is ethical, and the point of its employment is not to suggest that the world is so big that it takes a great deal of love to embrace it all, but that the world is so bad that it takes a great kind of love to love it at all, and much more to love it as God has loved it when He gave His son for it. The whole debate as to whether the love here celebrated distributes itself to each and every man that enters into the composition of the world, or terminates on the elect alone chosen out of the world, lies thus outside the immediate scope of the passage and does not supply any key to its interpretation. The passage was not intended to teach, and certainly does not teach, that God loves all men alike and visits each and every one alike with the same manifestations of His love: and as little was it intended to teach or does it teach that His love is confined to a few especially chosen individuals selected out of the world. What it is intended to do is to arouse in our hearts a wondering sense of the marvel and the mystery of the love of God for the sinful world—conceived, here, not quantitatively but qualitatively as, in its very distinguishing characteristic, sinful.[21]

An Abiding Knowledge and Experience

Finally, as simple as it may sound, God wants us to *know* that He loves us. He desires that now, as an essential part of our Christian growth, we *experience* in the fullest sense possible His love for us. This, I believe, is the meaning of Romans 5:5. Paul writes: "And hope does not disappoint us, because God has poured out his love into our hearts by the Holy Spirit, whom he has given us."

The NIV translation makes clear what the Greek text

21. Ibid., p. 516.

leaves ambiguous, namely, that "the love of God" referred to is *His* love for us and not ours for Him. The accuracy of the NIV is evident from two contextual considerations. First, "the love of God" is designed to be a proof of the security and certainty of our hope ("hope does not disappoint us, *because* . . ."). How can *our* loving God insure the fulfillment of our hope? On the contrary, since we are sinful and our love for Him often wanes and fluctuates, we could never have a sure hope. Paul's point, rather, is that we may be confident that our hope will not disappoint, will not bring us to shame, because *God*, even the God of all creation, *loves us*, and that immutably and irrevocably. Second, as is clear, verses 6–11 (linked up with v. 5 by the Greek word *gar*, "for") are an expansion on the nature of this love: a love of God *for us* as witnessed in the sending of His Son to die in our stead.

Paul's language is carefully chosen. He says that this love which God has for us is "poured out . . . into our hearts." The verb *poured out* is used in Scripture of the spilling of wine (Luke 5:37), the shedding of Christ's blood (Matt. 26:28), and the pouring out of the Holy Spirit at Pentecost (Acts 10:45). An even more graphic picture is painted by its usage in Acts 1:18 of the fate of Judas: "With the reward he got for his wickedness, Judas bought a field; there he fell headlong, his body burst open and all his intestines spilled out."

The force of the word in Romans 5:5 is similar to all of the above. Paul seeks to describe the unstinting lavishness with which God has flooded our hearts with a sense of His love for us. Murray says, "The hearts of believers are regarded as being suffused with the love of God; it controls and captivates their hearts."[22] "Like an overflowing stream in a thirsty land," writes Gifford, "so is the rich

---

22. Murray, *The Epistle to the Romans*, p. 165.

flood of divine love poured out and shed abroad in the heart."[23] Shedd calls it "an exuberant communication."[24] The love of God, quotes C. Hodge, "does not descend upon us as dew in drops, but as a stream which spreads itself abroad through the whole soul, filling it with the consciousness of his presence and favour."[25] The heart of the Christian is, so to speak, inundated by wave after wave of the love of God until one is overwhelmed by its majesty. Thus, as Packer says, "Paul is not talking of faint and fitful impressions, but of deep and overwhelming ones."[26]

Furthermore, Paul's use of the perfect tense is not without significance. God *"has* poured out" His love into our hearts. The perfect tense here implies, according to Packer,

> a settled state consequent upon a completed action. The thought is that knowledge of the love of God, having flooded our hearts, *fills them now,* just as a valley once flooded remains full of water. Paul assumes that all his readers, like himself, will be living in the enjoyment of a strong and abiding sense of God's love for them.[27]

Thus far I have simply assumed that Paul is describing our knowledge of the love God has for us in Christ. However, some insist that God's love in our hearts *is* the indwelling presence of the Holy Spirit. Whereas this is possible, I am inclined to believe that Paul is saying that the Holy Spirit evokes within our hearts the conviction, the spiritual sense, that God loves us. It is not the Holy Spirit *per se,* but the knowledge of God's love for us produced *by*

23. E. H. Gifford, *The Epistle of St. Paul to the Romans* (Minneapolis: The James Family Publishing, 1977), p. 112.

24. William G. T. Shedd, *A Critical and Doctrinal Commentary on the Epistle of St. Paul to the Romans* (Minneapolis: Klock & Klock Christian Publishers, 1978), p. 113.

25. Philippi, quoted by Charles Hodge, *Commentary on the Epistle to the Romans* (Grand Rapids: Wm. B. Eerdmans, 1974), p. 135.

26. J. I. Packer, *Knowing God* (Downers Grove: InterVarsity Press, 1973), p. 107.

27. Ibid.

the Holy Spirit that is in view (cf. 1 John 4:16). God's love as lavished upon us in Christ is seared into our religious consciousness as with a hot iron. Thus, as Cranfield explains, "the proof that our hope will not disappoint us in the end is the fact of the amazing generosity of God's love for us—a fact which we have been enabled to know and understand by the gift of His Spirit to us."[28]

28. C. E. B. Cranfield, *A Critical and Exegetical Commentary on the Epistle to the Romans* (Edinburgh: T. & T. Clark Limited, 1975), I:263.

Conclusion:

Rejoice in This Perfect Beauty!

B eauty" is a concept on which there is precious little agreement among philosophers and aestheticians. For example, whereas "objectivists" insist that beauty is an intrinsic property in things, "subjectivists" argue that beauty is only in the eye of the beholder. The former believe that things evoke pleasure because they are beautiful, whereas the latter contend that beauty *is* the pleasure that things evoke. Should the objectivist carry the day, as I believe he must, there is yet the problem of defining what constitutes beauty. Plato spoke of measure and proportion; Aristotle of order and magnitude. Aquinas, drawing on Augustine, argued that beauty consists of three properties: integrity or perfection, due proportion or harmony, and brilliance or clarity.

My reason for bringing up the subject of aesthetics in the conclusion to this study is that I believe it may properly be said, indeed *must* be said, that God alone is beautiful in an absolute and unqualified sense. All created reality, be it the raw elements of nature untouched by human hands or the paintings of Rembrandt, is beautiful in a derived sense and only to the degree that it reflects the perfections of God. In God alone are perfect order, harmony, magnitude, integrity, proportion, and brilliance. In Himself, independent of any benefit or blessing of His which we might enjoy, God is beautiful. There are no random brush strokes in the Divine Being, no clash of colors or dissonant sounds. God is aesthetically exquisite. There is in the Divine Being alone absolute resolution, integration, the utter absence of the slightest discordant element. He is, if I may so speak, the one impeccable painting on display in His works and Word, to be observed and adored. "One thing I ask of the LORD," said David; "this is what I seek: that I may dwell in the house of the LORD all the days of my life, *to gaze upon the beauty of the Lord* and to seek him in his temple" (Ps. 27:4; *emphasis mine*).

I can well remember the experience of awe-struck delight when first I saw Renoir's *Luncheon of the Boating Party*. I was not even sure how one was supposed to respond in the presence of a work of art such as this. I recall that its color, brilliance, proportion, and life evoked within me a sense of wonder and joy unlike anything I had known before. It is what philosophers refer to as aesthetic contemplation or disinterested delight. There were no questions of how I might benefit from the object or to what use it might be put to satisfy some ulterior desire. It was *just there*, to be appreciated, marvelled at, and adored.

Dare I say that in a sense this is what God desires of us? In His works and Word He has manifested Himself that we as His creatures might stand in awe, beholding the symmetry of His attributes, the harmony of His deeds, the glory of His goodness, the overwhelming and unfathomable grandeur of His greatness: in a word, *His beauty*. So often we turn to God only when in need. He is all too frequently for us no more than an instrument or tool subservient to our desires and put to use to achieve some selfish design. Of course, God *is* our source, our salvation, our sustenance. But He is first and fundamentally to be seen as altogether beautiful in Himself, worthy of all praise, glory, and honor were we never ourselves to profit from His goodness. Jonathan Edwards put it this way:

The first foundation of the delight a true saint has in God, is his [God's] own perfection; and the first foundation of the delight he has in Christ, is his [Christ's] own beauty; he appears in himself the chief among ten thousand, and altogether lovely: the way of salvation by Christ, is a delightful way to him, for the sweet and admirable manifestations of the divine perfections in it; the holy doctrines of the gospel, by which God is exalted and man abased, holiness honored and promoted, and sin greatly disgraced and discouraged, and free and sovereign love manifested; are glorious doctrines in his eyes, and sweet to his taste, prior to any conception of his interest in these things. Indeed the saints rejoice in their interest in God, and that Christ is theirs; and so they have great reason; but this is not the first spring of their joy: they first rejoice in God as glorious and excellent in himself, and then secondarily rejoice in it, that so glorious a God is theirs: they first have their hearts filled with sweetness, from the view of Christ's excellency, and the excellency of his grace, and the beauty of the way of salvation by him; and then they have a secondary joy, in that so excellent a Saviour, and such excellent grace is theirs.[1]

Simply put, God is infinitely splendid, and to Him is all glory due!

All that I have said in the preceding pages has had as its ultimate aim the presentation, inadequate though it be, of the beauty and glory of God. May He be the recipient of the adoring and ceaseless appreciation of His people, for what He is in Himself and for what He has done in Christ.

Sing to the LORD a new song; sing to the LORD, all the earth. Sing to the LORD, praise his name; proclaim his salvation day after day. Declare his glory among the nations, his marvelous deeds among all peoples. For great is the LORD and most worthy of praise; he is to be feared above all gods.

1. Jonathan Edwards, *Religious Affections*, edited by John E. Smith (New Haven: Yale University Press, 1969), p. 250.

For all the gods of the nations are idols, but the LORD made
the heavens. Splendor and majesty are before him; strength
and glory are in his sanctuary. Ascribe to the LORD, O
families of nations, ascribe to the LORD glory and strength.
Ascribe to the LORD the glory due his name; bring an
offering and come into his courts. Worship the LORD in the
splendor of his holiness; tremble before him, all the earth"
(Ps. 96:1–9).

Appendix A

The Development of Trinitarianism in the Early Church

 $\mathbf{I}$ t is probably fair to say that no doctrine of the Christian faith was subjected to as penetrating an analysis, both theologically and philosophically, as was the doctrine of God. Indeed, the first five hundred years of church history are intelligible only in light of the Trinitarian and Christological controversies and the conciliar declarations which they produced. My purpose here is not to present an exhaustive study on these developments but to highlight a few of the more significant events and individuals relevant to the emergence of a Trinitarian formula.

The history of Trinitarian thought in the early church falls into three stages. First, there is what I will refer to as the Pre-Nicene period, extending from the death of John the Apostle to A.D. 325. The second stage focuses on the climactic encounter between the teaching of Arius and Athanasius and the emergence of the Nicene Creed (A.D. 325). The Council of Nicea was not an exhaustive effort, but was purposely restricted in focus. Although

not addressed to the Trinitarian problem per se, the
Nicene Creed did declare the fundamental equality of
deity between Father and Son. Finally, in the Post-Nicene
period we see the debate take a decidedly Christological turn. The primary concern was to determine the
relation between the divine and human natures in the incarnate Son of God. In the process a Trinitarian construct
did emerge at Constantinople in 381 and the defini-
tive Christological statement took form at Chalcedon in
451.

I. Pre-Nicene Theology: The Development of Trinitarian Thought in the Age of Apologetics (A.D. 95–325)

A. The Post-Apostolic Fathers[1]

The post-apostolic fathers were thoroughly committed
to biblical monotheism. Their chief task was to embrace
the deity of Jesus without sacrificing that monotheistic
foundation which served to differentiate the early church
from paganism. However, no collective effort was made to
construct a theological formula by which the deity of
Christ might be reconciled with the affirmation that God is
one. On the whole, the post-apostolic fathers appear "as
witnesses to the traditional faith rather than interpreters
striving to understand it."[2]

The literature during this period contained little more
than a mere repetition of the biblical text with almost no

1. Chief among the post-apostolic fathers were Clement of Rome (who wrote
c. 90–100), Ignatius of Antioch (d. 117?), Polycarp of Smyrna (70–156), and Papias
of Hierapolis (60/70–130/140?). The more important literature of this period
includes *The Epistle of Barnabas* (138?), *The Epistle to Diognetus* (mid second
century), the *First* and *Second Epistles of Clement* (only the first of which was
written by Clement of Rome), *The Shepherd of Hermas* (early second century; in
which there is the suggestion of "binitarianism": the identification of the
pre-incarnate Christ with the Spirit), and the *Didache* (late first century).

2. J. N. D. Kelly, *Early Christian Doctrines* (New York: Harper & Row, 1960
[1958]), p. 90.

concern for theological explication. The fathers cite the biblical phraseology, explains Shedd, but

> without endeavouring to collect and combine the data of revelation into a systematic form. They invariably speak of Christ as divine; and make no distinction in their modes of thought and expression, between the deity of the Son and that of the Father. These immediate pupils of the Apostles enter into no speculative investigation of the doctrine of the Logos, and content themselves with the simplest and most common expressions respecting the triunity. In these expressions, however, the germs of the future scientific statement may be discovered.[3]

B. The Apologists[4]

The contribution of the apologists to the development of Trinitarianism came in the form of what has been called "Logos Christology." Justin Martyr, in his *Dialogue with Trypho*, may be taken as representative. Justin proposed that the pre-existent Christ was the "reason" or "intelligence" of God. This relationship between Christ and God was not personal, as if Son to Father. Rather, the pre-incarnate Christ (or, Word/Logos) was to the Father what rational thought is to the mind. Thus, on the analogy of a man whose thought is expressed verbally, the Logos (Word) of God assumed a physical form and became a man in Jesus Christ.

J. N. D. Kelly reminds us that for all the apologists, including Justin, "the description 'God the Father' connoted, not the first Person of the Holy Trinity, but the one Godhead considered as author of whatever exists;" and that "the generation of the Logos, and so His eligibility for

3. William G. T. Shedd, *A History of Christian Doctrine* (Minneapolis: Klock & Klock Christian Publishers, 1978 [1889]), I:265.

4. The more notable apologists include Justin Martyr (100–65), Quadratus (early second century), Aristides (early second century), Aristo (early second century), Tatian (110–72), Athenagoras (early second century), and Theophilus (late second century).

the title 'Son', [dated] not from His origination within the being of the Godhead, but from His emission or putting forth for the purposes of creation, revelation and redemption."[5] Therefore, whereas the apologists certainly did not conceive of the Divine Being as a Trinity of "persons," they did affirm an eternal and essential union of God and Logos. Similarly, "when Justin spoke of Him [the Logos] as a 'second God' worshipped 'in a secondary rank', and when all the Apologists stressed that His generation or emission resulted from an act of the Father's will, their object was not so much to subordinate Him as to safeguard the monotheism which they considered indispensable."[6]

C. Economic Trinitarianism

One of the more interesting developments in this period was that of "economic" trinitarianism. According to men such as Tertullian (d. 225) and Hippolytus (d. 236), we should conceive of God from two perspectives: first, as He is in Himself, without regard or relation to anything external to His own self-sufficient being, and second, as He is in relation to the world through the divine activities of creation, redemption and revelation.

With respect to the former, God is one, and yet contains within Himself His Word or Reason and Wisdom (on the analogy, again, of the mental functions in a man). As to the latter, His Word and Wisdom manifest themselves, respectively, as Son and Spirit. Thus in the "economy" (oikonomia; Latin, dispensatio) of God, that is to say, in the implementation of His eternal purpose in creation and redemption, God is three, revealing Himself as Father, Son, and Holy Spirit.

The Economic Trinitarians, however, insisted that the personal relationships of Father, Son, and Holy Spirit do

5. Kelly, Early Christian Doctrines, p. 100.
6. Ibid., p. 101.

not exist until, and only because of, the manifestation of God in creation and redemption. Prior to that time the distinctions are real, but *not personal.* Hence God is properly a Father and the Son properly the Son of this Father, not in the eternal being of God, but when manifested in the economy of His redemptive purpose for humanity. Tertullian even suggested that subsequent to the work of redemption and the creation of the new heavens and new earth the "Son" will recede into the Divine Being, still distinct in the constitution of the Godhead but not personally as "Son."

To his credit, Tertullian was the first to speak of the Godhead as a "trinity" *(trinitas),* and did not hesitate to describe both Son and Spirit as "persons" *(prosōpon).* But again, these are predications legitimate only in the temporal "economy," not in the eternal "being."

D. The Contribution of Origen (A.D. 185–254)

In contrast with both Tertullian and Hippolytus, Origen affirmed an *eternal* trinity of persons in the Godhead. In order to avoid the charge of tritheism, however, he insisted that the Father was the "fountain-head of deity," from whom the Son was in some sense "derived." The Son, he argued, is a "secondary God" *(deuteros theos).* The Son is God, but not in Himself; He is God by participation in the foundational deity of the Father. Origen thus explained the unity between Father and Son as one that corresponds, on analogy, to the unity between light and its brilliance; or again, between water and the steam that rises from it. "Different in form," explains Kelly, "both share the same essential nature; and if, in the strictest sense, the Father alone is God, that is not because the Son is not also God or does not possess the Godhead, but because, as Son, He possesses it by participation or derivatively."[7]

Thus it would seem that Origen moved a step closer to

7. Ibid., p. 130.

what would eventually become orthodox trinitarianism
when he affirmed an eternal distinction of persons
(hupostaseis) in the Godhead, but did so at the expense of
the consubstantiality of the Son with the Father, subordi-
nating the former to the latter.

E. Third-Century Anti-Trinitarianism

Earlier in our study we had occasion to discuss the
heresy of monarchianism, both in its "dynamic" and
"modalistic" forms. The reader should refer to that material in chapter three.

Summary

The reason for such divergent explanatory models of the
nature of God may well be found in the scriptural data to
which appeal was so often made. Jaroslav Pelikan has
identified four classes of Christological texts that bore
considerable influence in the early church.[8]

First, there are the passages of *adoption* which appear to
speak of a time when Jesus, who was at first only a man,
became divine, either at his baptism or resurrection.[9]

8. Jaroslav Pelikan, *The Christian Tradition: A History of the Development of
Doctrine. The Emergence of the Catholic Tradition (100–600)* (Chicago: University
of Chicago Press, 1971), p. 175.

9. The operative word here is "appear," for such texts do not in fact teach an
adoptionist Christology. Indeed, each class of texts here cited is theologically
compatible with all others. The hermeneutical abuse to which these texts were
subjected by heretical groups in the early church should not obscure the fact
that, although differing in emphasis and intent, they together constitute a
theologically unified portrait of our Lord. See C. F. D. Moule, *The Origin of
Christology* (Cambridge: Cambridge University Press, 1977), pp. 1–106; Benjamin
B. Warfield, *The Person and Work of Christ*, ed. by Samuel G. Craig (Philadelphia:
Presbyterian and Reformed Publishing Co., 1970); G. C. Berkouwer, *The Person of
Christ* (Grand Rapids: Wm. B. Eerdmans, 1973 [1954]) and David Wells, *The Person
of Christ: A Biblical and Historical Analysis of the Incarnation* (Westchester:
Crossway Books, 1984). For more popular but still helpful treatments of New
Testament Christology, see H. D. McDonald, *Jesus—Human and Divine* (Grand
Rapids: Zondervan, 1978 [1968]), and Leon Morris, *The Lord from Heaven: A study
of the New Testament teaching on the deity and humanity of Jesus Christ* (Downers
Grove: InterVarsity Press, 1974 [1958]).

Those texts most frequently cited in this regard are Psalm 2:7; Acts 2:32–36; and Matthew 3:13–17.

Second, there are the passages of *identity*, which either predicate deity of the Son or apply to him texts and titles otherwise true only of YHWH. Among such are John 10:30; Hebrews 1:8; Romans 10:12–13.

Third, there are texts which appear to affirm a *distinction* between the Father and Son, such as Proverbs 8:22–31; Psalm 110:1; John 17.

Fourth, and finally, there are passages of *derivation*, "which, by referring to the Father as 'the greater' or using such titles as angel, Spirit, Logos, and Son, suggested that he 'came from God' and was in some sense less than God."[10]

The influence of these classes of texts may be expressed as in the figure 1.

II. The Council of Nicea (A.D. 325): The Contribution of Arius and Athanasius to the Development of Trinitarian Thought

A. Arius and His Theology

The issue that was to divide professing Christendom was painfully simple but eternally significant: was Jesus fully divine and of the same substance with the Father? Or was He but a creature, superior to the rest of us to be sure, but nevertheless ontologically other than God?

Arius was a presbyter over the church district of Baucalis in Alexandria. In response to a request by Alexander, bishop of Alexandria, to explain the Christological significance of Proverbs 8:22–31, Arius affirmed, among other things, that "the son, born of the Father before all time, created and constituted in being before all ages, did not exist before He was begotten." The fundamental theologi-

10. Pelikan, *Emergence of the Catholic Tradition,* p. 175.

FIGURE 1   **Theories of the Relationship
Between the Father and the Son**

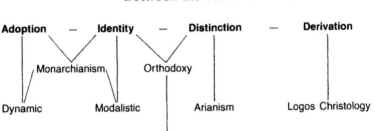

cal premise upon which Arius constructed his system was
a strict monotheism, according to which God, uniquely
transcendent, is the sole unoriginated source. From this,
Arius derived four conclusions concerning the Son.

First, the Son must be a creature, a product *ex nihilo* of
the divine will.

Second, inasmuch as the Son is a creature, He must have
had a beginning. "We are persecuted," cried Arius, "because we say the Son had a beginning whereas God [the
Father] is without beginning." Although the Son, unlike
other creatures, was created before the foundation of the
world, He was nonetheless "created." Hence, the Arian
slogan: "There was [a time] when He was not" *(ēn pote hote
ouk ēn).*

Third, the Son can have neither communion with nor
direct knowledge of the Father in any way other than that
which is true of all creatures (notwithstanding Matthew
11:25–30!).

Fourth, the Son, being a creature, is peccable, that is,
capable of both sin and change. Arius was cautious in
affirming this point and taught that "God in His providence foresaw that He [Christ] would remain virtuous by

His own steadfast resolution, and therefore bestowed this grace on Him in advance."[11]

On what basis, then, do the biblical authors refer to Jesus as "the Son of God"? According to Arius, this, as with all other Christological titles, was an expression of courtesy to the Son by virtue of his superior participation in the grace of God. The result of Arius' speculations was a reduction of the Son to a demigod, suspended between man and God, identical with neither but related to both. Nevertheless, the Arians persisted in worshiping the Son and praying to him.

Arius was excommunicated in 318 by the synod of Alexandria and was condemned by the synod of Antioch in 325. Again in 325 he was condemned by the Council of Nicea. He died in 336.

B. The Council of Nicea (A.D. 325)

This council was held in the city of Nicea, Bythinia, in Asia Minor, and met in 325 from May 20 to July 25.

There were essentially three parties in attendance: the Arians (led by Eusebius of Nicomedia, d. 341; Arius, not being a bishop, was unable to attend); the Homoousians (led by Alexander and a twenty-five-year-old Athanasius), whose label was a reflection of their conviction that the Son was of the same substance (homoousios; and the Latin equivalent, consubstantialis) and not merely similar to (homoiousios) that of the Father;[12] and finally, a large uncommitted body led by Eusebius of Caesarea.

The creed adopted by the council, with its unmistakably anti-Arian emphasis, reads as follows:

---

11. Kelly, Early Christian Doctrines, p. 229.

12. The difference between the two words (homoousios and homoiousios) is in a solitary letter. The difference between the two concepts of Christ is immeasurable. There are times in the history of the church when splitting theological hairs yields eternal consequences.

We believe in one God, the Father almighty, maker of all things, visible and invisible;

And in one Lord Jesus Christ, the Son of God, begotten from the Father, only-begotten, that is, from the substance of the Father, God from God, light from light, true God from true God, begotten not made, the same substance with the Father (*homoousion tō patri*), through whom all things came into being, things in heaven and things on earth, Who because of us men and because of our salvation came down and became incarnate, becoming man, suffered and rose again on the third day, ascended to the heavens, and will come to judge the living and the dead;

And in the Holy Spirit.

But as for those who say, There was when He was not, and, before being born He was not, and that He came into existence out of nothing, or who assert that the Son of God is from a different hypostasis or substance, or is created, or is subject to alteration or change—these the Catholic Church anathematizes.

The use by the council of the word *homoousios* is of special importance. Shedd explains:

The time had now come, when silence on the highly metaphysical but vitally fundamental point of the *substance* of the second Person in the trinity could not be allowed. It was now necessary to employ a technical term that *could not by any possibility* be explained or tortured into an Arian signification. The term *homoousios* could not by any ingenuity be made to teach anything but that the essence of the Son is one and identical with that of the Father; and this placed him in the same grade of *uncreated* being with the Father, and made him *autotheos* [God in himself].[13]

The purpose of the Creed should not be misunderstood. It was not designed to explain the trinitarian relationships

13. Shedd, A *History of Christian Doctrine*, I:311.

among Father, Son, and Holy Spirit. Neither was it designed to make sense of the relation between the divine and human natures in the person of Christ. The intent of its authors was simply to affirm without equivocation the full and consubstantial deity of the Son.

C. Athanasius and His Theology

The career and contribution of Athanasius (A.D. 300-73) are more directly related to the aftermath of the Nicene Council than to the events that preceded it. The Arian party experienced a remarkable resurgence over the next fifty years, during which time Athanasius was deposed and exiled on five occasions! His perseverance, both personally and theologically, has placed the church of Jesus Christ forever in his debt.

The theological starting point for Athanasius was noticeably different from that of Arius. The latter began with a rigid monarchian emphasis according to which the divine nature was both indivisible and incommunicable. Hence, the Son must be a creature. Athanasius, on the other hand, took his cue from the doctrine of redemption and concluded that only God Himself could save fallen humanity. From this he deduced an identity of nature between Father and Son. Athanasius insisted that the pre-incarnate Son is "other-natured" (heteroousios) with regard to mankind but "same-natured" (homoousios) with regard to the Father. The Son is thus co-equal and co-eternal with the Father.

Once again the necessity of theological precision, especially in the terms we use, is in evidence. "The distinction between homo ('same') and homoi ('similar') may seem trivial," notes Harold Brown, "but it was not so subtle that most ordinary Christians failed to grasp what is at stake. If Jesus is of the same substance as the Father, then he is truly God, and it is reasonable to think that he is able to 'save . . . to the uttermost' those who come to him (Heb. 7:25).

On the other hand, if he is only of similar substance, which was all that even the conservative Arians were willing to concede, then it is not evident that he necessarily possesses the divine power and authority he needs to make an atonement on behalf of the whole human race."[14]

III. Post-Nicene Theology: Constantinople (381), Chalcedon (451) and the Consolidation of Trinitarian Doctrine

A. *Constantinople* (A.D. *381)*

In the years following the Council of Nicea, Athanasius was actively engaged in formulating a theology of the Holy Spirit. Although he refrains from directly calling the Spirit "God," he insists that the Spirit, like the Son, shares one and the same substance *(homoousios)* with the Father. "If Athanasius took the lead in defending the *homoousion* of the Spirit," notes Kelly, "the task was completed, cautiously and circumspectly, by the Cappadocian fathers."[15]

Basil, bishop of Caesarea in Cappadocia, known as the "Great" (300–79); his younger brother Gregory, who became bishop of the small town of Nyssa (335–94); and Gregory of Nazianzus, who briefly occupied the patriarchal see of Constantinople (329–89) are known to history as "The Cappadocians." Following the lead of Athanasius, they affirmed and demonstrated the *homoousion* of the Spirit (Gregory of Nazianzus was bolder in his assertion of the Spirit's deity and consubstantiality than either of the two brothers).

It was at Constantinople in 381 that their theological efforts were decisive. The Nicene faith was reaffirmed and the consubstantiality of both Son and Spirit endorsed. What proved of lasting significance was the terminology

14. Harold O. J. Brown, *Heresies: The Image of Christ in the Mirror of Heresy and Orthodoxy from the Apostles to the Present* (Garden City: Doubleday, 1984), p. 119.

15. Kelly, *Early Christian Doctrines*, p. 258.

used to express the nature of the inter-trinitarian relation-ships. Heretofore the terms *ousia* and *hypostasis*[16] had been used synonymously. But as Justo González points out, both terms were ambiguous,

> for they referred to the individual subsistence of a thing as well as to the common essence of which all the members of the same species participate. The Cappadocians distin-guished between these two terms, reserving the use of *hypostasis* to refer to the individual subsistence of a thing, and that of *ousia* to refer to the essence that is common to the various members of a species. Then they affirmed that there are in God three *hypostases* and only one *ousia* or, in other words, three individual subsistences that participate in one divine essence.[17]

One final contribution of the Cappadocian fathers was their opposition to the teaching of Apollinaris (310–90), bishop of Laodicea, friend of Athanasius, and stalwart defender of the Nicene Creed.

B. Apollinaris and his Theology

It was certainly not for his advocacy of the deity of Christ that they opposed him, but rather for his tendency to reduce the reality of the human nature in the incarnate Son. Apollinaris insisted that to predicate of Christ two complete natures, one human and one divine, necessarily entailed a double personality. His rather ingenious alter-native was based on an appeal to the trichotomist view of man as allegedly taught in 1 Thessalonians 5:23. According to Apollinaris, the *soul* was the impersonal and uncon-

16. For an enlightening discussion of the history of these terms in the development of trinitarian thought, see Gerald Bray, *Creeds, Councils and Christ* (Downers Grove: InterVarsity Press, 1984), pp. 84–91, 149–51; and Brown, *Here-sies*, pp. 127–31.

17. Justo L. González, *A History of Christian Thought. Volume I. From the Beginning to the Council of Chalcedon* (Nashville: Abingdon Press, 1970), pp. 294–95.

scious vital principle that gives life to the *body*. The *spirit*, however, is the seat of personality, conscience, and rational thought. If Christ were conceived as lacking a human spirit, so reasoned Apollinaris, there would be in Him no sphere in which freedom of choice could be exercised, no human personality with which the divine Logos must be somehow united. Thus, Apollinaris suggested that the pre-incarnate Christ or Logos simply took the place of the human spirit. Christ is human, therefore, because His *body* and *soul* are human. But He does not have a human *mind/spirit*. His reasoning faculty, and thus the focus or seat of His personality, is the Word, the second person of the divine Trinity. Any possibility of conflict between two distinct intelligences in the incarnate Christ was thus eliminated. His sinlessness, of great concern to Apollinaris, was also thereby secured.

Of course, as Kelly reminds us, if Christ's humanity lacked the most characteristic element of human nature, the rational faculty, "His alleged manhood was not in the strictest sense human, but must have been something monstrous; it is absurd to call Him a man at all, since He was not a man according to the accepted definition."[18]

Apollinaris' teaching was condemned at Rome in 377, at Antioch in 378, at Constantinople in 381, and again at Rome in 382. The Council of Chalcedon in 451 was explicit in its rejection of Apollinarianism.

It is at this stage in the development of trinitarian thought that another decisive turn is taken. Heretofore, the efforts of the orthodox had been directed at two issues: (1) the fullness of Christ's deity and humanity, as witnessed in the repudiation of both Arius and Apollinaris, and (2) the relationship in the Godhead among Father, Son, and Holy Spirit. As regards the latter, there was recognized that which is common to all (essence; *ousia;* Latin, *substantia)* and that which is distinctive or proper to each (person;

18. Kelly, *Early Christian Doctrines,* p. 296.

hypostasis or *prosōpon;* Latin, *persona).* It yet remained, however, to determine and explain, if possible, the relationship between the human and the divine in the incarnate Christ. It was to this task that the sharpest minds of the age turned their attention.

C. Chalcedon (A.D. 451)

The Council of Chalcedon was the culmination to a debate that at times was as much political and personal as theological.[19] The principal characters in the dispute were *Nestorius* (d. 451), patriarch of Constantinople and representative of the school of Antioch (who was influenced in the formulation of his Christology by Theodore of Mopsuestia, d. 428, student of Diodore of Tarsus, d. 394), and *Cyril* (d. 444), patriarch and representative of the school of Alexandria.

At risk of oversimplifying an undeniably complex dispute, the general emphases of each school may be summed up as follows, according to J. F. Bethune-Baker:

> The mystic tendency was to be found at Alexandria, the rational at Antioch. The theologians of Alexandria fixed their attention almost entirely on the divine element in the person of Christ, and so asserted in the strongest terms the unity of the divine and the human in him. While confessing the duality, they emphasized the unity. The human nature was taken into organic union almost as if it were absorbed with the divine: though the union was a mystery, incomprehensible. By the teachers of the school of Antioch, on the other hand, attention was concentrated in the first place on the human element. The completeness of the

19. See R. V. Sellers, *The Council of Chalcedon: A Historical and Doctrinal Survey* (London: S P C K, 1961 [1953]). The best available treatment of our subject in English is still that of Aloys Grillmeier, S. J., *Christ in Christian Tradition. Volume One. From the Apostolic Age to Chalcedon (451)*, trans. by John Bowden (Atlanta: John Knox Press, 1975 [1965]). See also Bernard Lonergan, *The Way to Nicea: The Dialectical Development of Trinitarian Theology*, trans. by Conn O'Donovan (Philadelphia: Westminster Press, 1976).

human nature of the Lord was certain, even if its separate personality was thereby implied. The tendency at Antioch was thus to separate the natures and explain the separation—to confess the unity but emphasize the duality.[20]

According to Nestorius, the humanity of Christ was the temple in which the Deity resided. The relationship between the two natures was at best a "conjunction" or "connection." Cyril, on the other hand, insisted that, whereas prior to the incarnation there were two natures, subsequent to it there was but one. The union of the divine and human in Christ was natural, the latter frequently conceived as disappearing in the former. Thus, Nestorius balked at the title "God-bearer" (theotokos) for Mary, insisting that the title failed to emphasize that the child in Mary's womb possessed a human nature as well as a divine nature. "God-bearer" (theotokos) was permissible, then, only if she likewise was declared "man-bearer" (anthrōpotokos; Nestorius actually preferred the title "Christ-bearer" or christotokos). Cyril, as one would expect, believed the title "God-bearer" to be entirely appropriate.

The Council of Chalcedon followed on the heels of a series of convocations that served only to polarize yet further the personal and political barriers between the participants in the debate. In 431, at the Council of Ephesus, Cyril was successful in securing a condemnation of Nestorius, who subsequently retired into obscurity. The dispute, however, was far from over. Eutyches (d. 454), whom Kelly describes as an "aged and muddle-headed archimandrite,"[21] was condemned at the Synod of Con-

20. J. F. Bethune-Baker, An Introduction to the Early History of Christian Doctrine: to the time of the Council of Chalcedon (London: Methuen & Co. Ltd., 1951 [1903]), p. 255.
21. Kelly, Early Christian Doctrines, p. 331.

stantinople in 448 for advocating an extreme version of Cyril's doctrine of the one nature in Christ. Although his view is anything but clear, he was accused (unjustly?[22]) of teaching that Christ's humanity had been wholly absorbed by the Deity.

Flavian, the patriarch of Constantinople who had secured the condemnation of Eutyches, petitioned Pope Leo of Rome for support of his action. Although Eutyches likewise appealed to the Holy See, Leo responded (June 13, 449) with what has come to be known as the *Tome*, a document that denounced Eutyches, affirmed that the incarnate Christ was one person with two natures, and later served as a model for the Christological formula at Chalcedon. Eutychianism, however, was to make one final stand.

Dioscorus (d. 454), successor to Cyril, induced Emperor Theodosius II to summon a general council at Ephesus in 449 (known to history as the "Robber's Synod"). Leo's *Tome* was supposed to have been read and approved. But Dioscorus, acting as chairman of the council, rejected the document, reinstated Eutyches, harassed and imprisoned Leo's delegates, and "stole" an apparent victory· for the Alexandrians. Infuriated by this turn of events, Leo convened another council in Chalcedon (near Nicea in Asia Minor). The council met on October 8, 451, with over 500 bishops in attendance.

Among other things, the Chalcedonian Creed sought to preserve the best and reject the worst in both schools of thought. It reaffirmed the Nicene faith, approved Leo's *Tome*, and proceeded to describe the relationship of the divine and human in Christ as follows:

> We, then, following the holy Fathers, all with one consent, teach men to confess one and the same Son, our Lord Jesus

22. Ibid., pp. 332–34.

Christ, the same perfect in Godhead and also perfect in manhood; truly God and truly man, of a reasonable soul and body; consubstantial with the Father according to the Godhead, and consubstantial with us according to the Manhood; in all things like unto us, without sin; begotten before all ages of the Father according to the Godhead, and in these latter days, for us and for our salvation, born of the Virgin Mary, the Mother of God, according to the Manhood; one and the same Christ, Son, Lord, Only-begotten, to be acknowledged in two natures, inconfusedly, unchangeably [a corrective to the extremes of Cyril], indivisibly, insepara-bly [a corrective to the extremes of Nestorius]; the distinc-tion of natures being by no means taken away by the union, but rather the property of each nature being preserved, and concurring in one Person and one Subsistence, not parted or divided into two persons, but one and the same Son, and only begotten, God the Word, the Lord Jesus Christ, as the prophets from the beginning (have declared) concerning him, and the Lord Jesus Christ himself has taught us, and the Creed of the holy Fathers has handed down to us.

This creed thus affirmed that God and man had come together in the incarnate Christ, but without explain-ing precisely *how.* On the one hand, it rejected a dual-ism of natures in which the divine and human are joined but not united. On the other hand, it likewise re-sisted the tendency to fuse the two natures such that might result in a *tertium quid,* neither truly human nor divine.

Chalcedon, therefore, was both negative and positive in its emphasis. As to the former, it served to protect the church against the heretical extremes of either Antioch or Alexandria. The creed set boundaries, as it were, beyond which Christological speculation should not venture. As G. C. Berkouwer has put it, the Chalcedonian "pronounce-ment is comparable to a double row of lightbeacons which mark off the navigable water in between and warn against

FIGURE 2 **Issues Resolved at Constantinople and Chalcedon**

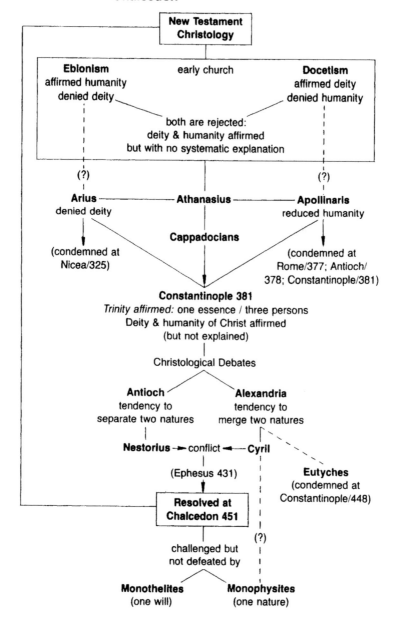

the dangers which threaten to the left and to the right."[23] The creed thus attempted to steer the early church between the Scylla of Antioch and the Charybdis of Alexandria.

On a more positive note, Chalcedon provided the early church with an exceptionally accurate description of the incarnate Christ as He is portrayed in the pages of the New Testament. Whereas it did not purport to be an exhaustive account of the person of Christ, it did provide a model by which both His humanity and deity might be intelligibly united in the one person. This is not to say that Chalcedon is final; but neither is it dispensable. Nothing *less* in our description of Christ can be permitted, but something *more* may well be within our theological reach. Simply put, the Chalcedonian statement is a sufficient minimum but by no means a theologically authoritative maximum.[24]

In conclusion, it must be admitted that the developments we have examined which culminated in the assertions at both Constantinople and Chalcedon are not easily digested. It may then prove helpful to attempt a visual overview of the preceding material (see figure 2).

23. Berkouwer, *The Person of Christ*, p. 85. See also Gerald Bray, "Can we dispense with Chalcedon?" *Themelios* 3 (January 1978):2-9; and Craig A. Blaising, "Chalcedon and Christology: A 1530th Anniversary," *Bibliotheca Sacra* 138 (October-December 1981):326–37.

24. Two misguided efforts to improve upon the Chalcedonian formula were made by the *monophysites* (who insisted on one nature in the incarnate Christ, and were condemned at the second Council of Constantinople in 553) and the *monothelites* (who advocated a variant form of monophysitism which insisted that Christ had but one will; condemned at the third Council of Constantinople in 680).

Appendix B

The Sovereignty of God and Process Theism

The threat of process theism to a biblically controlled and theologically coherent doctrine of God cannot be denied. This was made all too clear to me on reading Royce Gruenler's devastating and altogether convincing critique of process thought, *The Inexhaustible God: Biblical Faith and the Challenge of Process Theism* (Grand Rapids: Baker Book House, 1983).

Gruenler's work carefully identifies and assesses the principal themes in process thought: that God is neither immutable nor omniscient, neither transcendent nor sovereign, wholly dependent upon the universe in *its* becoming for *His* becoming, who literally (and not simply metaphorically) experiences process and development, more an ever-dependent recipient of the world than a sovereign contributor to its direction and destiny, and therefore Himself evolving, as it were, into that more complete being which, apart from the universe, He otherwise would not have become.

What is of special significance in Gruenler's analysis of process theism is what he perceives, correctly I believe, to be the underlying motive for its promulgation and popularity. Whereas process theism masquerades as a "theodicy," i.e., as an attempt to solve the problem of evil, it is in fact an "anthropodicy," a subtle but very real effort "to protect human freedom against the threat of a sovereign God."[1] Process theism, says Gruenler, is "primarily an essay in defense of human freedom, an anthropodicy, the ever recurring attempt of *homo curvus* to claim independence of the sovereign God who has revealed himself in Scripture as both Savior and Judge of the cosmic order."[2]

Gruenler describes his participation in a panel discussion on process theism to which both evangelicals and non-evangelicals contributed. He notes the concern he felt "to see how attractive the school [process thought] appears to be to a number of evangelical scholars, especially those of Arminian backgrounds whose heritage has emphasized the freedom of the individual to choose above the sovereignty of God over creation."[3] The reason is simple enough: if God is restricted to time, as process thought insists, and thus is incapable of seeing beyond His own immediate presence, far less able to foreordain or providentially superintend the events of history, the contingency and autonomy of human volition is preserved intact. But, as Gruenler correctly points out, much of the appeal in this concept of God rests on a misunderstanding of what biblical freedom entails. Freedom in the Old Testament and New Testament, he explains,

> is not defined as autonomous power apart from God, but rather as the creature's willingness to be faithful and selfless in service to God and to Jesus Christ. True Christian freedom is always to choose Christ, but one cannot choose Christ until God graciously removes the veil of rebellious nature. For if one has a nature, and the nature is

1. Royce Gordon Gruenler, *The Inexhaustible God: Biblical Faith and the Challenge of Process Theism* (Grand Rapids: Baker Book House, 1983), p. 8.

2. Ibid., p. 196.

3. Ibid., p. 38.

fallen (a very biblical view, as Romans 3:9–20 attests), is he really free to choose good? If he is not determined by his fallen nature, then his "I" has no substantial identity; that is, he is whatever he chooses to be at any moment, and thus is merely a succession of "I's." That is the process, but not the biblical view.[4]

The implications of the process view of God and human freedom are nowhere better in evidence than in the recent work of Terence E. Fretheim, *The Suffering of God: An Old Testament Perspective* (Philadelphia: Fortress Press, 1984). Fretheim does not explicitly affirm the tenets of process theism but believes that process studies "promise important new developments in the understanding of the God of the Old Testament, perhaps especially in a shift away from traditional formulations regarding the divine attributes."[5] When reading his description of divine foreknowledge one cannot help but believe that Fretheim has indeed joined hands with process thinkers in an attempt to reconstruct the concept of God in the Old Testament.

For example, Fretheim insists that texts which allegedly imply uncertainty on God's part concerning the response to His prophetic word are not accommodations on the part of the infinite for the sake of the finite, but literal declarations of *divine ignorance*. Notwithstanding the great storehouse of knowledge God has accumulated from past experience, He is incapable of predicting the future in detail. If it were the case that God infallibly knew His people would pursue course X rather than Y antecedent to His command that they pursue Y rather than X, He is lacking integrity; indeed, He is downright deceitful. That God should commit Himself to this or that course of action *if* His people respond as He commands must mean that

4. Ibid., p. 39–40.

5. Terence E. Fretheim, *The Suffering of God: An Old Testament Perspective* (Philadelphia: Fortress Press, 1984), p. 33.

God does not know how they will respond, otherwise His word "is both pointless and a deception."[6] In what way, then, is God different from men in respect of knowledge? Only in that He is able "to delineate all of the possibilities of the future in the likelihood of their occurrence in view of a thoroughgoing knowledge of the past and present."[7] That God should be portrayed as consulting with His people as to future activity or even as asking of them a question relative to certain future possibilities, is again proof, says Fretheim that "the future will bring new knowledge for God."[8] In brief, God will "learn."[9]

Fretheim concedes that God's knowledge of the psalmist (Ps. 139) is certainly wonderful, but nonetheless limited with respect to the future. And Isaiah's declaration of the greatness of God's knowledge in 40:28 and His predictions of the future "only claim that God knows what *God* will do in the future, and that God will accomplish God's purposes."[10] But one cannot help but wonder how God can know what God will do if what God will do is determined by and dependent on what *man* will do, which doing God does *not* know. It seems that God can at best hazard a guess at what He will do based on probabilities and percentages derived from His vast knowledge of past performances by His people. But is it really the case that the divine perspective on the "not yet" differs from the human only in that God, by virtue of His superior memory of the past, is able to calculate the likelihood of future events with a greater degree of precision? Fretheim view's God at best as a "divine bookie," setting odds on the probability of what might occur based on patterns of what has already transpired.

Now it is not my purpose here to challenge Fretheim

6. Ibid., p. 48.
7. Ibid.
8. Ibid., p. 56.
9. Ibid.
10. Ibid., p. 57.

and other process thinkers on the interpretation of individual texts such as Psalm 139 and Isaiah 40. In the first place, I have already dealt with the biblical evidence for divine omniscience (chp. 4) and omnipotence (chp. 6). Furthermore, there are available several excellent critiques of process thought in general, the best of which is the book by Gruenler.[11] But more important still, I do not believe that the issue separating process theism from classical biblical theism is of an exegetical or even hermeneutical nature. Rather, it is *theological*. With Gruenler, I am convinced that the underlying motive for the process interpretation of certain texts is the desire to secure for man a substantial measure of volitional autonomy vis á vis his relation to God. It is the desire to liberate man from the control of a sovereign God before whom the nations are but a speck on the scales (Isa. 40:15), a God who, from His heavenly throne, does whatever He pleases (Ps. 115:3), a God who changes the times and epochs, removes and establishes kings (Dan. 2:21), a God in whose hand the heart of the king is like channels of water to be turned wherever He wishes (Prov. 21:1), a God who does according to His will in the host of heaven and among the inhabitants of earth, whose hand no one can stay, a God to whom no one, not even the process theist, can say "what hast thou done?" (Dan. 4:35).

Thus the responsible exegete is confronted with two lines of evidence in the Scriptures. On the one hand are the assertions that God is omniscient, omnipotent, and absolutely sovereign in His determination of the course, character, and conclusion of human history. On the other hand we are repeatedly faced with the fact that human action is both meaningful and responsible. How is one to

11. In addition to Gruenler, see Ronald Nash, *Concept of God*, pp. 19–36; Bruce A. Demarest, "Process Trinitarianism," in *Perspectives on Evangelical Theology*, pp. 15–16; and Norman L. Geisler, "Process Theology," in *Tensions in Contemporary Theology*, eds. Stanley N. Gundry and Alan F. Johnson (Chicago: Moody Press, 1976), pp. 235–84.

reconcile these apparently conflicting assertions? Should one accept both as equally inspired declarations and simply acquiesce to the resultant mystery, trusting in the sufficiency of an infinitely powerful and wise God to so constitute and orchestrate the created order such that both are true? Or do we heed the call of process thought and gut the divine essence of those attributes apart from which the classical Christian concept of God cannot survive? Do we humbly submit to what is admittedly a theological paradox or arrogantly repudiate the revelation God has made of His will and ways and insist that He sacrifice His sovereignty at the altar of our autonomy?

Process theism, specifically that of Lewis Ford, whom Gruenler here has in mind,

> dismisses the one key to a proper interpretation of a biblical story, and that is the necessity of accepting biblical bipolarity on its own terms, that is, the scriptural declaration that God is all-powerful (e.g., "Does evil befall a city, unless the Lord has done it?" [Amos 3:6b]) and divine appeal to human responsibility ("Seek good, and not evil, that you may live" [Amos 5:14]). This is biblical merismus, a part here and a part there, and is enormously important in understanding the biblical paradox of polarities. God is sovereign *and* we are responsible secondary agents. Equivocating on either point does not do justice to genuine biblical bipolarity.[12]

To the charge of Ford (and Fretheim as well) that if God is omniscient and sovereign over the world He is morally responsible for its evil, Gruenler asks: responsible to whom or what?

> The sovereign Lord of the Old Testament is the one who *defines* evil: he is not the one who must himself be obedient to some higher good which is sovereign over him. Good and

12. Gruenler, *Inexhaustible God*, p. 166.